Feminist Theory, Crime, and Social Justice

About the Theoretical Criminology Series

The Theoretical Criminology series consists of short-format content on some of the best cross-disciplinary studies focusing on contemporary theory and thought from across the social sciences and humanities, all specifically designed to meet the needs of the criminal justice community. Each work is designed to provide students and scholars with a rigorous introduction to the theory or perspective under consideration as well as its direct implications for the way we think about issues of crime and justice. Students and instructors wishing to add theoretical enrichment to their courses and studies can add these digestible, inexpensive works to their reading lists, bringing insight and understanding from the world of social science and humanities to that of criminal justice.

Other Books in the Series

Frank Tannenbaum and the Making of a Convict Criminologist by Matthew G. Yeager, Forthcoming

Capitalism and Criminal Justice by Peter B. Kraska and John Brent, Forthcoming

Feminist Theory, Crime, and Social Justice

Alana Van Gundy

Series Editor

Victor E. Kappeler

ELSEVIER

AMSTERDAM • BOSTON • HEIDELBERG • LONDON
NEW YORK • OXFORD • PARIS • SAN DIEGO
SAN FRANCISCO • SINGAPORE • SYDNEY • TOKYO
Anderson Publishing is an imprint of Elsevier

Anderson Publishing is an imprint of Elsevier
The Boulevard, Langford Lane, Kidlington, Oxford, OX5 1GB, UK
225 Wyman Street, Waltham, MA 02451, USA

First published 2014

British Library Cataloguing in Publication Data
A catalogue record for this book is available from the British Library

Library of Congress Cataloging-in-Publication Data
A catalog record for this book is available from the Library of Congress

ISBN: 978-0-323-24274-5

For information on all Anderson publications
visit our website at **store.elsevier.com**

Printed and bound by CPI Group (UK) Ltd, Croydon, CR0 4YY
Transferred to digital print 2013

This book has been manufactured using Print On Demand technology. Each copy is produced to order and is limited to black ink. The online version of this book will show color figures where appropriate.

DEDICATION

To P.H.

Thank you for being decent when no one else was.

To Levi

Until we meet again. Always, my love.

CONTENTS

CHAPTER *1*

Feminist Theory and Social Justice

We all fight over what the label 'feminism' means, but for me it's about empowerment. It's not about being more powerful than men—it's about having equal rights with protection, support, justice. It's about very basic things. It's not a badge like a fashion item.

Annie Lennox

Feminist theory provides a framework that allows for consideration of the unique social positioning and life experiences of women. An interest in feminism and feminist theory re-emerged in the 1960s and 1970s, and the field is currently in a postmodernist phase. Viewing crime and justice from a feminist perspective enables theorists to examine the impact that variables such as race, age, social standing, oppression, and patriarchy have on the relationship between women, crime and criminality, and social justice. Current criminological theory is premised on a male model of criminal justice and does not capture the impact of mechanisms of social control on women nor the unique life histories, risk predictors, or needs of women in the criminal justice system. Utilization of a theoretically-based gender-specific model of criminality allows for examination of the mechanisms and factors specific to gender as a means to attain social justice for women.

1.1 DEFINITION AND FORMS OF FEMINIST THEORY

Feminist theory is a broad, generalized system of ideas about society, social life, and humanity that was developed from the standpoint of women. It focuses on the social, emotional, biological, and psychological experiences of women and society and is female-centered in three primary ways: its investigation starts with the experiences of women in society, women are the central focus of the theory, and that it is critical to produce "a better world for women" (Lengermann & Niebrugge-Brantley, 2000, p. 443). Feminist theory can be interpreted in a multitude of ways, but the core of any feminist theory must describe and explain the tenets of the social world experienced by women, apply questions, thoughts, and ideas to improve the social world for women, and consider the intersection of additional demographic variables such as age, race/ethnicity, and social standing (Hooks, 1984; Lengerman & Niebrugge-Brantley, 2000).

Interpretation of feminist theory has led scholars and academics to dissect the breadth of feminist theory into six primary forms: liberal, traditional Marxist, radical feminism, socialist feminism, postmodern, and critical race feminism. *Liberal feminist* theory focuses on pro-scribed gender roles, the patriarchal division of labor in work and family, and the impact of gender roles on social, legal, political, and economic equality. The theoretical premise of liberal feminism is based upon the social contract theories of the sixteenth and seventeenth centuries, meaning that the natural and legal rights of women must be protected in order to maintain an organized society. Liberal feminists argue that women are equal to men as they both possess the inherent human capacity for reasoning and moral agency. One key area of emphasis for liberal feminist theorists is equality of opportunity—in particular, gender equality with regards to education, economics, and politics. Additionally, they focus on the codification of universal human rights, a restructuring of the division of labor within law, work, and family spheres, and the acceptance of individualism and personal choice.

Traditional Marxist feminist theory locates the origin of women's oppression not in individual opportunity but as inherent within a society's political and economic organization and structure. This view-point argues that women's subordinate position in society originated with the development of private property, capitalism, and the hege-mony of the ruling class. Marxist feminists argue that gender and class inequity are interrelated (but place emphasis on class) and that women's experiences of oppression must be understood as a direct power relationship between women and men. Marxist feminists believe, for example, that a woman working within the home constitu-tes a form of domestic slavery, that women's work is provided low compensation as a means of control and oppression, and that as long as society's structure is based on capitalist principles, women will remain a minority class.

The *radical feminist* viewpoint identifies male dominance, or patri-archy, as the root of gender inequality. Radical feminist theory has posited biology, heterosexuality, and social construction as intertwined with inequality and focuses on the relationships between the female and male gender in their analyses (Bunch, 1987; Firestone, 1970; Wittig, 1992). Radical feminists focus on social organization, gender and structural oppression, overt and covert forms of violence against women, components of socialist and psychoanalytical concepts, and the positive impacts that women have on society. The key differences between radical feminist theories and the other forms of feminist theory include the focus on the explicit tie to patriarchy and violence against women, the celebration of differences between women and men (in comparison to other theoretical viewpoints focused on equality), and suggested solutions such as the individual and societal rejection of patriarchy, emphasis on standing together as women, and importance of women learning their strength, independence, and knowing their value. Movements related to radical feminism include Black is Beautiful, the Dove sisterhood campaign, and Women Stand Together.

Socialist feminist theory views human nature and social equality as fluctuating with the control of the mode of production. Socialist feminists argue that a deep understanding of Marxism must be embraced, and that an extension of radical and Marxist theory is necessary to better understand the intersection of gender, class, and the integration between the two. Socialist-based feminist theorists focus on gender and class, but unlike Marxist theory, which ranks class as the most important variable, socialist feminists view gender and class as equally important. This framework views the relationship between class and gender as reciprocal and differs from Marxist feminist theory in four ways: it extends the meaning of material conditions to include more than the mode of production of goods (such as the use of the human body and the production of knowledge), emphasizes human subjectivity, analyzes interrelated variables (class, politics, economics, etc.), and suggests different solutions for change (Marxism calls for the end of capitalism and socialist feminists call for conscious mobilization to improve both macro- and micro-level conditions).

Postmodern feminists argue that sex and gender are socially constructed as a derivative of language. According to this theoretical viewpoint, gender ideals, norms, and categorizations are socially constructed and labeled by society. Of particular interest to postmodernist feminists is who is creating, defining, and interpreting these labels and categories of differences. Postmodernists resist categorization, black and white "truth," and terms or concepts such as crime, deviance, social control, and justice as socially created and not a universal "truth." They support moving the understanding of gender to the center of focus, deconstructing research and knowledge focused on women, and considering categories that trivialize or marginalize one gender in relation to another.

Lastly, *critical race feminist* theory's primary focus is on the intersection of gender and race. Critical race theorists focus on the "double" subordinate positions that women of color hold in society. In other words, women as a class are oppressed in the professional and personal spheres (access to leadership opportunities, sexual harassment, discrimination, and sexism, for example), and women of color face both gender-related and racial-related obstacles of oppression such as racism and minority discrimination. Feminists who identify as critical race theorists argue that there is not a social, economic, or political framework available to understand the multilayered and unique experiences of women of color and that this is necessary when studying the lives of women of color (Collins, 2000; Crenshaw, 1991; Hooks, 1984).

Each form of feminist theory provides a unique viewpoint of women with respect to their social standing, economic freedom, obstacles of oppression (sexism, racism, classism, and intersectionality, etc.), and life experiences. Feminist theories continue to provide a valuable framework for research in sociology, economics, psychology, education, political science, women's studies, criminology and deviance, and criminal justice. The feminist framework allows for a theoretical-based focus on gender differences, gender inequality, gender oppression, and structural oppression.

1.2 ORIGIN AND EVOLUTION OF FEMINISM AND FEMINIST THEORY

The first printed feminist works were published in the early fifteenth and sixteenth centuries. These writings focused on the important gendered roles that women have in society (De Pizan, 1405), the theological superiority of women, and female equality or lack thereof. In 1792, Mary Wollstonecraft published *A Vindication of the Rights of Women* and in 1918 another ground-breaking book was written by Marie Stopes: a sex manual titled *Married Love.* These works evidenced the clear discontent of women with their proscribed social, marital, and economic roles, in addition to the resultant social inequality.

Despite these early writings, feminist theory was not labeled or identified as such until much later in history. The origin of feminism and feminist theory has been traced in three eras, or waves, throughout history. First Wave feminism stemmed primarily from writings published in Canada, the United Kingdom, the Netherlands, and the United States. This wave focused on the struggle for women's political rights; in particular, it emphasized the right to vote. Two important dates emerged during the time of First Wave feminism: 1848, when the first Women's Rights Convention was held in Seneca, New York and 1920, when passage of the 19th Amendment ended women's suffrage in the United States. Throughout the era of First Wave feminism, women fought for and won the right to execute wills, the right to choose their professions and own property in their name, the legalization of divorce, the right to be granted custody of their children in a divorce, educational access, and the right to vote in an education setting.

Second Wave feminism began in the 1960s in the United States and is referred to as the Women's Liberation Movement. In 1963, Betty Friedan's *The Feminine Mystique* identified the issues, expectations, and roles that women play in society as "the problem that has no name," and Second Wave feminism turned its focus to sexuality and identity, family roles, workplace inequity, abortion rights, and the ability to control reproduction. This wave of feminism encapsulated the Equal Pay Laws and Equal Rights Amendment. Additionally, it established marital rape laws, domestic violence centers, aid for battered women, and the National Organization for Women.

Third Wave feminism began between 1980 and 1990 and is referred to as postmodern feminism. It originated as a backlash to critical deficiencies perceived throughout the era of Second Wave feminism. Four major theoretical perspectives contribute to postmodern feminism: intersectionality theory, postmodernist and poststructuralist approaches, global feminism, and the agenda of a new generation of younger feminists that were discontent with the previous state of feminist theory (Coleman, 2009). Third Wave feminist theorists reject the traditional idea of femininity and incorporate components of queer theory, transgender politics, intersections between race and gender, and individualist feminism in their studies of women.

Each wave of feminism significantly impacted the advancement of feminist theory. With the First Wave of feminism, theory and research focused on identifying inequality in areas such as employment and property ownership and examined social conditions from a liberal feminist and socialist feminist viewpoint. Second and Third Wave feminism integrated components of radical feminism, critical race feminism, and postmodernist feminism and extended mainstream theory to include intersectionality. At each stage, the evolving viewpoints faced resistance and were deemed "rebellious," and included foci on gender discrimination, subordination, stereotyping, sexual objectification, and the patriarchal nature of society.

1.3 STRENGTHS AND CRITICISMS OF FEMINIST THEORY

Feminist theory has been controversial from its inception. The theory provides a clear framework for examining the social positioning of women, calls for a reassessment of social structure and inequity, questions the origin and purpose of individual, government, and social/political power, and translates directly to policy implications and recommendations. Additionally, it has allowed for slow and evolutionary advancements within the economic, social, and political realm of women, and in particular nations it has resulted in legislation that advances the rights of women.

These changes and advancements in society have resulted in the emergence of important criticisms. One significant critique of feminist theory involves the definitions, components, and understanding of the theory itself. As first designed, components of feminist theory were defined in order to understand the plight of white women who were deemed to be disadvantaged because they were unable to access the universal "social positioning" that they hoped to attain. The definitions and concepts of feminist theory at that point offered no understanding of women from different cultures, socioeconomic classes, or social and economic positioning. This deficiency has been significantly advanced by the creation of critical race theory and women of color theory, but prior to this advancement, feminist theory best explained the eco-nomic, political, and social standing of white, middle-class women.

Additionally, the understanding of the main components of feminist theory itself, by proxy, categorizes gender divisions to use males as the reference point. This is necessary in particular instances, but in others, it impedes the level of explanation, understanding, and application in the contexts of women's lives. This has been directly addressed by fem-inist theorists within the postmodernist phase. Examining the social construction of gender has greatly eased the rigidity with which catego-ries of gender are measured; yet continuation of this work is imperative for advancement of feminist theory.

Another significant issue with feminist theory is that it comes in a multitude of forms. This can be deemed a benefit at times, but it also results in scattered research and a lack of uniformity in scientific understanding. For example, in addition to the six forms as discussed above, there also exists cultural feminism, lesbian feminism, and mate-rialist feminism. These different tenets of the theory often cause confu-sion to theorists, academics, and laypeople, and do not allow for the consistency necessary for systematic reviews and meta-analyses.

Additional criticisms were identified in Kathy Lay and James Daley's 2008 article entitled "A Critique of Feminist Theory." They argue that a review of empirical articles showed the wide range of stud-ies focused on feminist theory used the theory as a "lens for other issues" (p. 49) and did not focus on expanding the theory itself. Later, they state, "The greatest disappointment was the dearth of research actually focusing on refining feminist theory. Where were the studies that asserted the crucial components of feminist theory or sought to empirically test those components? Where were the studies that sought to add the additional confirmation of existing feminist theory ... we were surprised by the absence of critical scholarship on feminist theory development" (2007, p. 57). Lay and Daley suggest that scholarship that is focused on feminist issues must identify components of the the-ory, gather and provide empirical evidence testing theoretical compo-nents of each form of feminist theory, and focus specifically on theoretical advancement (2007).

These criticisms provide important points for theoretical advance-ment. Each branch of feminist theory is subject to multiple criticisms, but together they form a comprehensive and explanatory theory. For example, it has been argued that liberal feminism ignores social structure and class; radical feminism focuses on the class of sex when there is no evidence for a "sex class;" Marxist feminism focuses solely on class, and as capitalism will not be overthrown, it may not necessarily be the most useful framework with which to advocate change; and socialist feminism ignores the concepts of capitalism. Placed together, the strengths of these theories may be able to form the framework of an ultimate feminist theory that poses a better understanding of all women and advances the status of women throughout the world.

1.4 IMPACT OF FEMINIST THEORY ON THE VIEWPOINT, STATUS, AND CONCEPTS OF CRIME AND JUSTICE

Feminist theory offers valuable contributions to the field of criminology and criminal justice. The translation of feminism to the field of crime and deviance resulted in a field of study called feminist criminology. Feminist criminology is defined as "the body of criminological research and theory that situates the study of crime and criminal justice within a complex understanding that the social world is systematically shaped by relations of sex and gender" (Miller & Mullins, 2006, p. 218). It is an integrated and multifaceted theoretical viewpoint that focuses on the concept of gender when examining crime, deviance, and criminality. The primary aim of feminist criminology is to produce a "distinctly feminist approach to crime and criminal justice" (Akers, 2000, p. 219).

Two early publications within the field of feminist criminology were Dorie Klein's "The Etiology of Female Crime" (1973) and Carol Smart's "Women, Crime, and Criminology: A Feminist Critique" in 1976. Both of these significant publications described and analyzed the history of the explanations of crime and identified gaps in those explanations. Essentially, they introduced the importance of non-biological explanations of crime and deviance (to include sociological and psychological explanations) to the criminal behavior of women. Their writings stimulated a theoretical movement that focused on reviewing the status of current theories, the state of female crime, and the lack of inclusion of relevant risk predictors pertinent to women. This early phase of feminist criminology aimed to critique criminological theory for not including gender differences and characterizing women in sexist ways, and called for empirical studies of gender and crime (Daly & Maher, 1998).

The most recent phase of feminist criminology parallels the current era of the feminist movement and stresses the need for understanding gender versus sex, sexual identity, race and ethnicity, culture, and the interactions between race and gender, and culture and gender, within the framework of methodological analyses. Feminist criminologists have started to focus on the problem of categorizing the term "women" as a unified category, acknowledging that women's experiences are formed by legal and criminological discourses, revisiting the relationship between sex and gender, and reflecting on the strengths and limitations of constructing truth and knowledge (Daly & Maher, 1998, p. 3).

Five elements must be considered by feminist criminologists in order to distinguish a feminist-based approach to criminological theory, from traditional criminological theory. They include (verbatim from Daly & Chesney-Lind, 1988, p. 504):

1. Gender is not a natural fact but a complex social, historical, and cultural product; it is related to, but not simply derived from, biological sex difference and reproductive capacities.
2. Gender and gender relations order social life and social institutions in fundamental ways.
3. Gender relations and constructs of masculinity and femininity are not symmetrical but are based on an organizing principle of men's superiority and social and political-economic dominance over women.
4. Systems of knowledge reflect men's views of the natural and social world; the production of knowledge is gendered.
5. Women should be at the center of intellectual inquiry, not peripheral, invisible, or appendages to men.

Merry Morash (2006) extends the integration of these five elements into gender-based studies through the identification of both macro and micro conceptualizations of gender. She states, "At the macro level— that is, within the global system, a country, or a society—whether people are women or men, girls or boys, affects social and economic status and opportunities and expectations in relation to education, work, family and leisure. Specifically, there are gender differences in monetary and other resources, in power, and in access to different kinds of jobs. The patterns of differences are referred to with different terms, including gender organization, the sex gender system, gender arrangements, and gender stratification" (p. 9). Conversely, the micro or individual level "involves a dynamic process of definition of appropriate characteristics and actions associated with being feminine or masculine...beliefs about characteristics and behaviors considered to be masculine or feminine are referred to as gender ideologies or gender definitions" (Morash, 2006, p. 9). Therefore, research must include an examination of socially-constructed micro and macro level gender variables as a way of appropriately encompassing and understanding the context of women's lives in relation to crime. In the context of criminology, this has led to what is termed the generality versus gender-specificity debate.

1.4.1 Generality versus Gender-Specificity

The generality versus gender-specificity debate revolves around the question "Does general criminological theory explain male and female criminality?" Stemming from the feminist movement and feminist criminology, it has been argued that the traditional, male-based models of criminological theory do not adequately capture female criminality. This concern has become of the utmost importance as female crime is changing in typology and increasing in number (Chesney-Lind, Morash, & Stevens, 2008; Steffensmeier & Allan, 1996). Those who argue that a general model of crime is adequate at explaining both male and female criminality utilize gender as a control variable, and do not consider gendered life history or gender-specific risk predictors in the statistical model. As a result, all individuals are classified and treated on the general model of criminality and delinquency. In contrast, those that support the use of a gender-specific model of criminology utilize gender-specific risk factors in analysis, consider gender a risk predictor and not a control variable (for both females and males), and argue that classification, programming, and treatment must be targeted toward an individual's gender.

In 1996, Darrell Steffensmeier and Emilie Allan published "Gender and Crime: Toward a Gendered Theory of Female Offending." The goal of their article was to advance criminological theory and research by providing a thorough review of the issues surrounding gender and crime. They provided statistics regarding the gender gap in crime (as discussed later in Chapter 2), examined traditional theories and their corresponding explanations of the gender gap in crime, and ultimately offered a constructive discussion of key elements that must be included in a gendered approach to criminality. These elements include: explanations of both female and male criminality by revealing how the organization of gender deters or shapes delinquency for both genders; theory should account for gender differences in type of crime, frequency of crime, and differences in context of offending; consideration of the female trajectory into crime and; explore the extent to which gender differences are attributed to social, historical, cultural, and biological and reproductive differences (Steffensmeier & Allan, 1996).

Consideration of gender in a theoretical model may take many forms. It could include gender-specific variations of the theoretical variables offered within a traditional model to combat inherent androgyny in criminological theory. It may also control for gender identity and gender roles. That is, if an individual is female but assumes or identifies with a male role, theoretical testing must account for that in order to appropriately measure the impact of gender on crime (in conjunction with the biological component of sex). An additional component of a gender-specific model is the utilization of the appropriate research methods. There are no hard and fast rules for feminist research methods *per se*, but there is a feminist approach to methodology. That approach includes examining femininity and masculinity, the use of qualitative and ethnographic analysis, a focus on reflexivity, and a minimization of distance and hierarchy among researchers and participants (Flavin, 2001).

Utilization of these gender-based methods (and lack thereof) has resulted in questions and concern about the ability of a general criminological model to appropriately measure female criminality. When traditional criminological theory is examined with a gender-based methodology, findings suggest that male-based explanations are inadequate at explaining female criminality. For example, Linda Tyler's feminist-based approach in 1997 included interviews of 26 women with at least one criminal conviction each. She found that her qualitative interview process allowed unique gender-specific risk predictors to emerge that had not yet been considered or tested for in traditional criminological theory. Specifically, problems with relationships such as self-abuse, sexual abuse, and domestic violence were found to significantly impact the risk of female criminality (Tyler, 1997).

Both the general model of crime and the gender-specific model of crime have empirical support. Karen Heimer's 1996 longitudinal study found that the general risk factors that were valid for females were also valid for males when measuring for theoretical components of differential association, deterrence, social control, social structural, and interactional theory. The only exception was relationships with peers; which evidenced a greater effect on females (Heimer, 1996). Similar support for a general approach to criminality was garnered for strain theory (Mazerolle, 1998), self-control (Burton, Cullen, Evans, Alarid, & Dunaway, 1998), and components of differential association and social control (Alarid, Burton, & Cullen, 2000).

Studies focusing on gender-specific risk predictors have also found support. The Mazerolle study referenced above found support for both a general model (strain variables) and a gender-specific model (prior delinquency, noxious neighborhood conditions). Spencer De Li and Doris Layton MacKenzie's 2003 study of adult social bonds also found support for a gender-specific model of criminality. They found that, of 125 individuals on probation, the male probationers reported being more likely to have a job, more likely to commit theft, robbery, or assault, and more likely to commit nondrug offenses than females. Additionally, they found that throughout a life course trajectory, social bonds (living with a spouse, attending school, having a job) hindered the criminal activity of male probationers but did not impact female adult offending (De Li & MacKenzie, 2003; Sampson & Laub 1990).

Findings on the generality versus the gender-specific models are mixed. One important consideration here is that these findings are testing traditional, male-based models of criminal behavior. By proxy, these models will best explain what is stereotypically considered to be *male* crime such as assault, rape, and homicide. Additional studies have pointed out that these models are not necessarily the most appropriate framework with which to test female criminality. The addition of variables such as social cognitive skills and cognitive transformation (Bennett, Farrington, & Huesmann, 2005; Giordano, Cernkovich, & Rudolph, 2002), social support and posttraumatic stress disorders (Andrews, Brewin, & Rose, 2003), particular relationship factors (Lo & Zhong, 2006), and beneficial female and peer friendships (McCarthy, Felmlee, & Hagan, 2004; Piquero, Gover, MacDonald, & Piquero, 2005), all have stronger effects on female delinquency, lending support to the concept of gender differences in criminal behavior.

1.4.2 Relationship Between Traditional Criminological Theory and Feminist Criminology

Criminological theory is separated into six primary categories of theories of crime causation. These include rational choice theory, trait theories (biosocial and psychological trait theories such as arousal or attachment theory), social structure theories (social disorganization, strain, and cultural deviance theory), social process theories (social learning and social control theories), developmental theories such as life course theory and latent trait theory, and social conflict and critical criminology (Marxist theory, power-control theory, and feminist theory).

The first five categories comprise the majority of academic research in criminology. They reflect the mainstream understanding of what impacts criminal behavior; biology, societal impact and structure, and psychology. The theories are also very succinct and offer easily operationalized variables. For example, Travis Hirschi's 1969 social bond theory has four elements: attachment, commitment, involvement, and belief. These four elements are further broken down into: attachment to family, friends, and community; commitment to future, career, success, and personal goals; involvement in school activities, sports, community organizations, religious groups, and social clubs; and belief in honesty, morality, fairness, patriotism, and responsibility. These variables are widely believed to be related to criminal behavior, and testing of the theory has found consistent support. Those that support a general theory of crime argue that these variables should be consistent across gender and those that argue for a gender-specific model argue that gender will mitigate the impact of these elements differently for females and males.

The last category of crime causation, social conflict, and critical criminology does not offer variables that are as widely supported. In areas where capitalism is heralded, few will support its negative attributes. Critical criminology can be traced back to the early 1800s, when Karl Marx, Willem Bonger, Ralf Dahrendorf, and George Vold's writings focused on oppressive structures, productive forces, social domination, and social conflict. The theories are, in short, unpopular given their economic and political implications and difficult to operationalize as official reports and traditional crime-related variables do not measure many areas of foci included in conflict and critical criminology (feelings of oppression, gender identity, patriarchy, etc.). Additionally, when the policy implications of the theory include societal accountability and a change in a capitalistic system, the theoretical implications appear politically problematic.

Situated outside of traditional criminology and as a tenet of critical criminology, critical feminist theory focuses on how capitalism and patriarchy render women economically subordinate, politically powerless, and sexually exploited. These foci help explain the prevalence of the non-serious and intrinsically focused crimes of women, the status offenses of young women, and the commodity crime of prostitution. John Hagan's power-control theory is an additional feminist model that uses the link between class position and family functions to explain the onset of female crime. This model integrates three important variables to culminate in a life course viewpoint that power relations are developed within the family (a patriarchal structure), reflect the power differentials that exist in the workforce, and impact children's propensity for criminality. The theory posits that young girls growing up in a patriarchal family fear legal sanctions more than males and are at risk for illegitimate behavior outlets such as running away, cutting, and suicide attempts. It also proposes that relationship-based power and control may interact with personal traits such as self-control, personality, and emotion to determine criminal propensity.

Traditional criminological theory does not consider the gender-related risk factors and variables as proposed by conflict criminology. Yet in 2008, Paul Mazerolle identified three reasons to do so. First, he argued that understanding female offending helps fulfill a criminological duty to advance the field and "illuminate the diversity of crime problems across groups and over time" (p. 2). Second, he argues that criminologists are "woefully inadequate if they cannot capture and explain female criminal behavior," and that theorists are taking a "leap of faith" to assume that traditional theory explains both male and female offending (p. 2). Since the time of his article, women's criminal behavior has become more violent and they are becoming incarcerated at higher rates, so his arguments should act as a warning to those dedicated to advancing criminology as a field. And third, he points to the impact that ignoring gender has on offender programming. He argues that not considering gender in criminal justice interventions is a challenge; and that challenge must be better studied in order to grasp the full picture of female criminality.

Traditional criminological theory is consistently analyzed and oftentimes supported. The "outsider" status of conflict theory calls to light important variables that are omitted in this analysis. These variables include the victimization experiences of women, sexualization of female delinquency, and the criminalization of survival strategies (Chesney-Lind, 1989); subordinate social status of women in a patriarchal society (Reckdenwald & Parker, 2008); intersectionality between race, gender, power, control, and crime (Burgess-Proctor, 2006; Schwartz, 1996; Sokoloff & Dupont, 2005); status, importance, and impact of primary relationships (Andrews et al., 2003; Piquero et al., 2005); after-effects of sexual trauma and abuse (Bloom, 2003; Bloom & Covington, 1998); the impact of domestic violence; self-injurious behavior such as cutting; single parenthood; social, sexual, and marital roles; and experiences with sexism and racism (Holsinger, 2000). Without situating these variables either within the framework of traditional criminological theory or in a feminist-based framework, feminist criminologists argue that traditional criminology is flawed, antiquated, and inadequate at understanding the relationship between gender and crime.

1.4.3 Impact of Feminist Theory on Crime and Justice
Despite a lack of support by mainstream criminologists, feminist criminology has impacted the viewpoints, status, and concepts in crime and justice in a multitude of ways. Crime has traditionally been viewed as a male activity, and theory, punitive measures, and the criminal justice system itself has been modeled on the male-based crime and delinquency model. Feminist criminology argues that this leads to the neglect, misclassification, and inappropriate punishment for women offenders. Viewing crime and justice from a feminist lens impacts the process of criminal justice itself, criminological theory, and public policy.

First, the process of criminal justice has been described as "gendered justice," meaning the process of justice is based upon the understanding of the male gender (Belknap, 2001; Chesney-Lind,

1988). This occurs at all steps of the criminal justice process, beginning with arrest and ending with aftercare. Traditionally, it has been suggested that there are variations in arrest patterns based upon gender, with women less likely to be arrested than men (Visher, 1983), differences in sentencing (Bernstein, Kelly, & Doyle, 1977; Chesney-Lind, 1973; Nagel, 1983; Nagel & Weitzman, 1971; Schlossman & Wallach, 1978; Simon, 1975), and differing experiences within the system of corrections (Chesney-Lind, 1973; Rafter, 1985; Rasche, 1974; Smart, 1976). Viewing these variations from a feminist theoretical approach will allow researchers to ask why these variations exist, how variables converge between race and gender to result in these differences, and to put mechanisms into place to ensure that women are appropriately classified, processed, and detained.

Second, the field of feminist criminology impacts criminological theory in numerous ways. The addition of gender and gender-specific variables will allow for more accurate statistical measurement of female crime and deviance. Related variables such as gender roles, gender organization, family relationships, mental health, sexual trauma history, and co-occurring medical disorders will provide a broader and more inclusive theory for all individuals, not just females. While the variables may evidence a stronger relationship with females, consistent with feminist literature, including measures of both masculinity and femininity will greater encompass the general picture of crime. Inclusion of the feminist approach to criminology may conceptually strengthen the current criminological theory and result in a gender-based theory that appropriately predicts the crime and criminal behavior of those that identify with the female gender role.

Third, the field of feminist criminology greatly impacts public policy. Including gender-specific components in theoretical analysis will result in a deeper understanding of female crime. This understanding translates directly to public policy in terms of service provision (appropriate classification instruments, jail and prison facilities, and gender-specific programming, for example), policing (understanding of life history and officer attitudes toward women offenders), and incarceration (the use of community-based corrections for nonviolent female offenders and alternatives to imprisonment). Feminist criminology implies that to address female crime and criminality, the system of patriarchy should fundamentally be changed or abolished; legislation must be created that protects women from victimization in the forms of intimate partner violence, trauma, and exploitation; that criminal justice reform must be implemented at all levels (police, courts, corrections); and that social support and community-based alternatives will better serve female offenders (Akers, 2000; Chesney-Lind, 1989; Logan, 2008). Implementing any of these public policy changes for female offenders will raise awareness of the state of female crime and directly impact the offenders themselves (both current and future offenders), society, and the community at large.

1.5 SOCIAL JUSTICE

Barry Levy and Victor Sidel (2005) state that "Social justice embodies the vision of a society that is equitable and in which all members are physically and psychologically safe. Social justice also demands that all people have a right to basic human dignity and to have their basic economic needs met. Our commitment to social justice recognizes that health is affected by a host of social factors. It is not possible to address trauma and violence without also wrestling with poverty, racism, sexism, classism, homophobia and all other forms of stigma. Because of this, we cannot ignore deep-seated inequalities as we seek answers to problems like violence and trauma" (p. 8). In simple terms, social justice is the view that everyone should have equality in the form of economic, educational, political, and social rights and opportunities.

Social justice exists when all people share a common humanity, support equitable treatment and human rights, and fairly allocate community resources. People are not to be discriminated against, nor their welfare and well-being constrained or prejudiced on the basis of gender, sexuality, religion, political affiliations, age, race, belief, disability, location, social class, socioeconomic circumstances, or other characteristic of background or group membership. John Rawl's *Justice as Fairness* (1971) and David Miller's *Principles of Social Justice* theory (1999) have both expanded on this form of social justice.

1.5.1 Justice as Fairness
In 1971, John Rawls posited the "justice as fairness" theory. The core tenets of this theory revolve around the idea of a social contract, in which people freely enter into a social agreement to follow a set of

rules and principles for the betterment of society despite the implications of the rules on the individual. In other words, collective society becomes more important than individualistic needs and gains. Rawl's theory of justice as fairness has two primary principles. First, every person has the same right to equal and basic liberties (micro level), and these equal and basic liberties are compatible with the liberties for all (macro level). Second, social and economic inequalities must satisfy two conditions. First, they are attached to an office or position open to all, instead of a specific individual. And second, they are to directly benefit the least advantaged of society (Rawls, 1971). He considers the least advantaged to be those that lack the following:

- The basic rights and liberties such as freedom of thought and liberty of conscience
- Freedom of movement and free choice of occupation against a background of diverse opportunities
- Powers and prerogatives of office and position of authority and responsibility
- Income and wealth
- Social bases of self-respect.

Rawls argues that the principles of justice must be applied in a four-stage sequence:

1. adoption of the principles to regulate society
2. constitutional convention, which dictates processes of governance
3. just and fair laws are enacted
4. appropriate and equal application of the rules by administrators, the interpretation of the constitution and laws by the judiciary, and the following of the rules by all members of society (1971, p. 15).

He argues that "A just world order is perhaps best seen as a society of peoples, each people maintaining a well-ordered and decent political (domestic) regime, not necessarily democratic but fully respecting basic human rights" (2003, p. 5). The theory of justice as fairness can be used as a framework to determine if current society and its processes and outcomes evidence social justice as outlined.

1.5.2 Principles of Social Justice
David Miller's 1999 *Principles of Social Justice* offers a pluralistic theory (in comparison to Rawl's unified theory of one measure of social

justice) built around humanistic principles that guide everyday life and focuses on the importance of social context. Miller's theory of social justice focuses on the distribution of advantage and disadvantage in society. Advantages include money, property, jobs, education, medical and child care, honors, awards and prizes, and personal security, while the disadvantages consist of dangerous work and military and governmental service (1999, p. 10).

His theory focuses on three main elements of social justice: need, desert, and equality. He posits that "Need is a claim that one is lacking basic necessities and is being harmed or is in danger of being harmed and/or that one's function is being impeded. Desert is a claim that one has earned reward based on performance, that superior performance should attract superior recognition. Equality refers to the social ideal that society regards and treats its citizens as equals, and that benefits such as certain rights should be distributed equally" (1999, pp. 207, 210, 134, 141, 232). Miller does not emphasize one of the three elements more than another as he argues the pluralist notion of the theory allows humans to equally balance and decide which is more important based on the social context of any given situation.

The principles of both Rawl's and Miller's theories have been utilized in many areas. For example, the University of St. Thomas School of Social Work presents the following 10 principles for their Social Work for Social Justice Principles (verbatim from University of St. Thomas, 2013):

1. Human dignity—dignity of the human person is the ethical foundation of a moral society. The measure of every institution is whether it threatens or enhances the life and dignity of a human person.
2. Dignity of work and the rights of workers—in a marketplace where profit often takes precedence over the dignity and rights of workers, it is important to recognize that the economy must serve the people, not the other way around. If the dignity of work is to be protected, the basic rights of workers must be respected—the right to productive work, to decent and fair wage, to organize and join unions, to private property, and to economic initiative.
3. Community and the common good—the way in which society is organized in education, economics, politics, government—directly affects the human dignity and the common good.

4. Solidarity—we are our brother's and sister's keepers. We are one human family, whatever our national, racial, ethnic, economic, and ideological differences.
5. Rights and responsibilities—human dignity is protected and health community can be achieved only if human rights are protected and responsibilities are met. Every person has a fundamental right to things necessary for human decency. Corresponding to these rights are responsibilities to family, community, and society.
6. Stewardship—it is incumbent upon us to recognize and protect the value of all people and all resources on our planet. While rights to personal property are recognized, these rights are not unconditional and are secondary to the best interest of the common good especially in relation to the right of all individuals to meet their basic needs.
7. Priority for the poor and vulnerable—a basic moral test of any community or society is the way in which the most vulnerable members are faring. In a society characterized by deepening divisions between rich and poor, the needs of those most at risk should be considered a priority.
8. Governance/principle of subsidiarity—governance structures in all levels/settings have an imperative to promote human dignity, protect human rights, and build the common good. While the principle of subsidiarity calls for the functions of governments to be performed at the lowest level possible in order to insure for self-determination and empowerment, higher levels of government have the responsibility to provide leadership and set policy in the best interest of the common good.
9. Participation—all people have a right to participate in the economic, political, and cultural life of society. Social justice and human dignity require that all people be assured a minimum level of participation in the community. It is the ultimate injustice for a person or a group to be excluded unfairly.
10. Promotion of peace—peace is the fruit of justice and is dependent upon the respect and cooperation between peoples and nations.

1.6 FEMINIST THEORY, CRIME, AND SOCIAL JUSTICE

Feminism and feminist criminology were both developed on the premise that social justice is not societally supported or available for females. The feminist framework integrates seamlessly with the field of social justice as the goal of both theoretical viewpoints is to attain social, economic, political, and educational equality for all individuals. Arising from discontent with the stagnation of the field of feminism, researchers and feminists have been meeting regularly over the last few years and have established what is called the New Women's Movement Initiative (NWMI). The NWMI has expressed frustration with the current feminist movement's lack of advancement initiative. Throughout conversations and dialogue, the NWMI has established the basis of their movement on what they term social justice feminism.

A study conducted by Linda Burnham entitled "The Absence of a Gender Justice Framework in Social Justice Organizing" interviewed 11 individuals from the NWMI and found the following problems as identified by NWMI members (verbatim from Burnham, 2008):

1. A gender justice lens is rarely incorporated into the work of mixed-gender social justice organizations.
2. The absence of a gender justice lens may be attributed to the subordination of sexism as a legitimate concern among "competing ism-s;" the absence of a sense of urgency on gender issues; the lack of accessible gender analysis and training tools; and the negative reputation of the feminist movement, among other factors.
3. There are multiple negative consequences to the absence of a gender justice lens in social justice organizing, including the neglect of key issues and constituencies; the mishandling of sexist gender dynamics, including sexual harassment; the disaffection and silencing of women leaders; and the development of sexually biased campaigns.
4. To develop a social justice movement that consistently incorporates a gender justice lens into its vision requires that activists build the will and a sense of urgency; demonstrate that gender sensitive organizing is more effective; share the experiences of model organizations and campaigns; provide gender education and training; and promote women's leadership.

Burnham's recommendations for organizations that use a feminist social justice framework are directly applicable to the current state of criminology. Her recommendations include:

• Motivate social justice leaders to consistently incorporate a gender justice lens in their framework.

- Develop and provide tools for gender justice education, training program planning, and program evaluation.
- Promote and support women's leadership.
- Provide resources to support the incorporation of a gender justice framework in social justice organizing.

In addition, her appendices outline what she terms the principles of social justice feminism. They include: center social justice feminism around those that are particularly vulnerable; integrate markers of social inequality such as race, class, sexuality, nationality, citizenship, and ability; recognize power conditions in general society and within the women's movement; actively challenge racism, heterosexist bias and class privilege; intentionally include those impacted by public policy in the creation of the policy; seek alliances and partnerships with organizations outside of the women's movement (including organizations that do not identify as feminists); and recognize that the struggle for gendered justice is global, and worldwide organizations must be included (Burnham, 2008, p. 16).

Support for Burnham's point is provided in Kristin Kalsem and Verna Williams' 2010 Law Publication article. They provide the history of the NWMI and suggest that in order to "sow the seeds of social justice feminism" (p. 164) the following must be done: be productive, think creatively and think big, be constructive and advance the field in a different manner than has been attempted previously, re-envision those included in promoting the greater ideals of the movement, increase recognition of interlocking subordinating structures (race, ethnicity, age, etc.), ask important questions to identify diversified opinions and thoughts, allow for healing through sharing experiences and concern, and develop solutions from a "bottom-up" approach (p. 183).

Components of social justice and feminism integrate well into the current viewpoint of women's crime. The principles of social justice would dictate that we as a society need to collectively recognize that women are affected by a host of factors, and those factors are often different than the factors that affect men. Those factors must be identified and utilized in theoretical testing so that society can better prevent, treat, and respond to female criminality. The deep-seated patriarchal nature of society has resulted in the invisibility of women in society that is reflected in the system of criminal justice.

Implementing social justice would mean that criminology and society need to make those women visible; that is, place them at the forefront of research and create a model unique to their needs.

Rawl's justice as fairness model would argue that because collective society is of more importance than individualism, female offenders must be addressed collectively and in the way that most aids them and their unique, gender-specific needs. This will collectively strengthen the field of criminology, not only for women, but for all individuals involved in crime and the society that regulates their behavior. His argument that resources and positions must be open to the least disadvantaged directly translates to the concept that women that are victimized, traumatized, and engaged in criminal behavior must be provided gender-specific and appropriate programs in order to become productive members of society and successfully reintegrate.

Miller's principles of dignity, community, solidarity, responsibility, stewardship, and priority for the vulnerable are important concepts for criminology to consider in conjunction with Burnham's principles for feminist social justice. Viewing women as those that are at a distinct disadvantage and that show a need according to Miller (the rates of victimization experienced by females dictates a clear propensity for being harmed) is not popular, but it is necessary. Without this viewpoint, the crime rates of women, the lack of understanding of gender-specific risk factors, and the resistance from those that choose not to advance will continue to stymie the field. Feminist criminologists have found themselves in the same position of the NWMI—discontent with the stagnation and calling for a need for theoretical development and advancement.

CHAPTER 2

Crime Typology and the Gender Gap

Man is defined as a human being and a woman as a female - whenever she behaves as a human being she is said to imitate the male.

Simone de Beauvoir

Females and males commit different types and amounts of crime according to official crime and victimization statistics. Historically, females have engaged in less serious forms of criminal activity, and a large majority of all criminal activity has been committed by males. In particular, males are traditionally more likely to engage in aggressive, assaultive, and serious forms of crime such as murder, rape, and robbery. While these trends are supported by official statistics, important changes in these trends have been noted with regards to gender and criminal behavior.

This chapter will first identify the primary differences in criminal offense typology by gender, present supporting statistics, and introduce what is termed the "gender gap" in crime. Next, a discussion will be presented on how traditional criminological theory explains the gender gap in comparison to how feminist criminology views it. The chapter will then focus on the direct implications of viewing crime, criminality, and the gender gap from both the traditional and feminist criminological viewpoints. It will conclude with a discussion tying the gender gap in crime to components of social justice.

2.1 CRIMINAL OFFENSES

Males and females evidence different levels of criminal activity as measured by arrest, self-report, and victimization data. Males and females are both more likely to be involved in nonserious criminality rather than serious criminality, but males are more likely than females to engage in criminal activity in all official crime report categories with the exception of prostitution. When comparing across gender, women have traditionally been more likely to commit non-violent crimes, such as fraud, shoplifting, and prostitution, than males. With regards to violent crime, females are more likely to commit a violent crime against someone they have a relationship history with (spouse, child, friends, etc.), and males more often target violent offenses toward strangers. These measures are consistent throughout the Uniform Crime Report, the National Crime Victimization Survey, and official arrest statistics.

Table 2.1 presents support for these findings from the Uniform Crime Report, using the percent of total arrests for the years 2000, 2005, and 2011. Table 2.1 shows that over an 11-year time span of reporting, males are far more likely to be arrested for both violent and property crime. Males comprise almost all arrests for murder, nonnegligent manslaughter, and forcible rape, and comprise the majority of arrests for all crimes with the exception of prostitution and embezzlement (in which they are equally likely to be arrested as females). The next-closest arrest levels are for fraud, forgery and counterfeiting, larceny/theft, disorderly conduct, and liquor violations. Similar findings are presented by Pollock (2002), Lauritsen, Heimer, and Lynch (2009), and Britton (2011).

2.2 THE GENDER GAP

The gender gap in crime refers to the aforementioned differences in the number and types of crimes committed by males and females. As presented in Table 2.1, official arrest statistics show that men and women evidence a gender-specific propensity for being arrested for engaging in specific forms of crime. Additionally, they are charged, prosecuted, and sentenced at different rates (conflicting support is provided for women being sentenced in a harsher manner for violating gender norms, for example). These differences have led to a gender gap in criminal offending rates, court sentencing, and rates of incarceration. This gap has held over time, but academics and researchers have speculated that this gap is converging. For example, between 1960 and 1970, when female arrest rates of larceny, fraud, forgery, embezzlement, and robbery increased, female crime was said to be narrowing the gender gap (Noblit & Burcart 1976; Simon, 1975). Support for these findings regarding larceny, embezzlement, and fraud were later reiterated by Steffensmeier and Cobb (1981) and Steffensmeier and Allan (1996) (measurement period was between 1935 and 1990). The gender gap has narrowed primarily with respect to property (intrinsically based crime) and violent offenses.

Table 2.1 Percentage Arrests by Gender

Crime	2000		2005		2011	
	Females	Males	Females	Males	Females	Males
Murder and nonnegligent manslaughter	11	89	11	89	12	88
Forcible rape	1	99	2	98	1	99
Robbery	10	90	11	89	12	88
Aggravated assault	20	80	21	79	23	77
Burglary	13	87	15	86	16	84
Larceny/theft	36	64	39	61	43	56
Motor vehicle theft	16	84	18	82	18	82
Arson	15	85	17	83	18	82
Other assaults	23	77	25	75	27	72
Forgery and counterfeiting	39	61	40	60	38	62
Fraud	45	55	46	55	41	59
Embezzlement	50	50	50	50	50	50
Stolen property	17	83	20	81	20	80
Vandalism	16	85	17	83	19	81
Weapons	8	93	8	92	8	92
Prostitution	62	38	66	34	69	31
Sex offenses	7	93	8	92	8	93
Drug abuse	18	82	19	81	20	80
Gambling	11	89	9	91	12	88
Offenses against the family and children	22	78	24	76	25	75
Driving under the influence	16	84	19	81	25	75
Drunkenness	13	87	15	85	18	82
Disorderly conduct	23	77	26	74	28	72
Vagrancy	21	79	21	79	19	80
All other offenses	21	79	23	77	25	76
Suspicion	20	80	14	86	22	78
Curfew and loitering	31	69	30	70	30	70
Total	22	78	23	76	26	74

Source: Uniform Crime Reports, 2000, 2005, and 2011 (Washington, DC: US Department of Justice).

While official arrest statistics show that differences in crime typology occur by gender, arrest and conviction rates over time also support the idea of gender differences. Additionally, they show the rapid increase in female crime. As Table 2.2 presents, over time, females have steadily become more likely to be arrested for robbery,

Table 2.2 Percentage of Arrests by Gender Evidencing Trend of Gender Gap over Time

Crime	1980 Females	1980 Males	1995 Females	1995 Males	2011 Females	2011 Males
Murder and nonnegligent manslaughter	13	87	10	90	12	88
Forcible rape	1	99	1	99	1	99
Robbery	7	93	9	91	12	88
Aggravated assault	13	87	18	82	23	77
Burglary	6	94	11	89	16	84
Larceny/theft	30	70	33	67	43	56
Motor vehicle theft	9	91	13	87	18	82
Arson	12	88	16	84	18	82
Other assaults	14	86	20	80	27	72
Forgery and counterfeiting	32	68	36	64	38	62
Fraud	41	59	41	59	41	59
Embezzlement	28	72	44	56	50	50
Stolen property	11	89	14	86	20	80
Vandalism	9	91	14	86	19	81
Weapons	7	93	8	92	8	92
Prostitution	69	31	61	39	69	31
Sex offenses	8	92	8	92	8	93
Drug abuse	13	87	17	83	20	80
Gambling	10	90	15	85	12	88
Offenses against the family and children	17	83	20	80	25	75
Driving under the influence	10	90	15	85	25	75
Liquor laws	15	85	19	81	30	70
Drunkenness	8	92	12	88	18	82
Disorderly conduct	16	84	22	78	28	72
Vagrancy	14	86	19	81	19	80
All other offenses	15	85	18	82	25	76
Suspicion	14	86	15	85	22	78
Curfew and loitering	23	77	30	70	30	70
Total	16	84	20	80	26	74

Source: Uniform Crime Reports, 1988, 1995, and 2011 (Washington, DC: US Department of Justice).

aggravated assaults, burglary, larceny/theft, motor vehicle theft, arson, other assaults, forgery and counterfeiting, embezzlement, theft of property, vandalism, prostitution, drug abuse, offenses against family and children, driving under the influence, liquor laws, drunkenness, disorderly conduct, and suspicion. Female arrests have remained stable for forcible rape, fraud, weapons, sex offenses, vagrancy, and curfew and loitering and show a decrease in arrests for gambling. In comparison, all categories of percentage of arrests for males have decreased with the exception of forcible rape (remains stable), fraud, weapons, sex offenses, gambling, and curfew and loitering.

Table 2.2 also provides the documentation of the long-term gender gap in crime. Traditional criminology and society alike show a lack of concern with the level of female engagement in criminal activity. Yet, over the years, the total crime rate of women has steadily increased. In 1980, for example, women comprised 16% of total arrests. In 1995, that percentage increased to 20% and by 2011, it rose to 26%. It is important to note that the Uniform Crime Report official statistics above only reflect adult offending, but juvenile arrest statistics mirror the converging trends:

- Between 1989 and 1993, juvenile female arrests increased by 23% in comparison to an 11% increase in male offending.
- During this same time frame, females were responsible for 17% of the increase in juvenile arrests for violent crimes, cases involving juvenile females with delinquency offenses increased by 31%, and the juvenile female custody population increased from 16% to 29% of all detained juvenile offenders.
- Between 1983 and 1993, juvenile female arrests increased by 3% (from 21% to 24%).
- Despite these increases, delinquency cases involving juvenile females were less likely to be formally processed, more likely to receive probation, and less likely to be placed in detention (Yamagata & Butts, 1996).

The convergence of increasing female crime and decreasing male crime has resulted in the gender gap slowly narrowing. In 2009, Lauritsen, Heimer, and Lynch published an article in *Criminology* that focused on this narrowing gap and in particular, examined earlier violent offending. While previous studies utilized data from the Uniform Crime Report or the earlier National Crime Victimization Survey, their study examined data from the National Crime Survey and the National Crime Victimization Survey between the years of 1973 and 2005. Their analysis provided support for the narrowing of the gender gap for aggravated assault, robbery, and simple assault. When examining why this gap was narrowing, they provided support for the argument that significant contributions to the convergence of male and female crime were not solely due to the increase in female crime, but also due to the decrease in male crime (Lauritsen et al., 2009). Support for the narrowing of the gender gap has also been provided by multiple studies (Austin, 1982; Lauritsen et al., 2009; Nagal & Hagan, 1983; Schwartz, 2008; Schwartz & Rookey, 2008; Schwartz, Steffensmeier, Zhong, & Ackerman, 2009; Zimmerman and Messner, 2010).

While support exists for this narrowing gender gap in criminal behavior, it has raised controversy. The debate over the convergence of male and female crime began in 1975 when Freda Adler and Rita Simon proffered two primary questions in separate publications. First, is there really a convergence in crime? And second, if there is a convergence, what are the causes? Official report data does evidence that female crime is increasing and that male crime is decreasing, but opposing sides to the convergence theorists argue that this does not mean that male and female crime is converging. In addition, they argue that the way official crime is measured does not accurately reflect all forms of female criminality. Therefore, researchers focused on gender-based crime rates argue that the concept of the converging gender gap in crime is not accurate. This debate has resulted in important advances regarding the need to focus on appropriate crime typologies utilizing different forms of data sources to form an accurate picture of male and female criminality, and the importance of chosen study methodology.

In 2002, Meda Chesney-Lind and Joanne Belknap analyzed patterns in young girls' rates of delinquency. They provide strong evidence for an argument that girls' and boys' crime rates evidence a convergence in particular crime typologies according to official data sources, but that self-report data "fail to show the dramatic changes found in official statistics during either the eighties or the nineties" (p. 4). Citing Center for Disease Control statistics from the Youth Risk Survey, the National Youth Study, the Denver Youth Survey, and research from San Francisco and Canada (Corrado, Odgers, & Cohen, 2000); they argue that girls' levels of aggression and violence have not changed, but the trends in official statistics reflect changes in law enforcement practices, the relabeling of female crime, and changes in gender role and norm expectations (Chesney-Lind & Belknap, 2002).

In 1999, Robert O'Brien published a study in the *Journal of Quantitative Criminology* that looked at the long-term trends in arrest rates for 1960–1995. His article presented a critical analysis of previous methods utilized to examine the gender gap and pointed out that up to the time of his research, all but one study utilized a few years of data, interval data, or averaged annual data. Additionally, studies finding support for the convergence in crime trends across genders had employed methodology that did not provide significance levels, correct for auto-correlation, or use appropriate methods (p. 98, 99). He conducted a time-series data analysis to address these shortcomings and utilized statistics provided by the Uniform Crime Reports for Part I crimes only (homicide, robbery, aggravated assault, burglary, larceny, and motor vehicle theft). He found that convergence of crime rates occurred for robbery, burglary, and motor vehicle theft, diverged for homicide, and aggravated assault and larceny remained stable over the 35-year time frame (p. 111, 112).

Chen and Giles (2004) also conducted a time-series analysis on crime rates, but their data was gathered from the CANSIM II databank collected by Statistics Canada in 2002. They examined criminal charges of adult females and males in Canada from 1983 to 2000 (a more direct measure than the measures of arrest used in previous studies). Their results suggest that "the results of any tests for gender convergence might differ according to the type of crime in question" (p. 597) and they found convergence in 12 of the 20 variables tested. They found no convergence in the gender gap with regards to murder, robbery, other violent crimes, stolen goods, frauds, and federal statutes. Convergence occurred for attempted murder, manslaughter, property crimes, breaking and entering, motor vehicle theft, over and under theft, other crimes, prostitution, gaming and betting, offensive weapons, and other criminal codes (Chen & Giles, 2004, p. 597). This study provided important expansion for methodologists and international measurements, and mixed support for the convergence model based upon a more direct measure of charges, thus controlling for any possible gender bias which may exist in the arrest process.

In other words, the convergence debate within criminology is centrally focused on whether or not official statistics report an accurate portrait of the amount of crime that females commit. This debate is again tiptoeing around the question of whether or not the current measurement system that we have in place is primarily only applicable to male offenders. If, for example, females commit relational offenses such as bullying or gossiping, but it is not an officially measured crime, the measures as they exist do not adequately capture the delinquent behavior of women, but simply the law-violating behavior of women. Female crime appears to be increasing according to official statistics. This debate questions if this is indeed the case, or if the system of measurement lacks (and has lacked since its inception) the appropriate means to understand and gather an accurate portrait of female criminality. Additionally, it calls to question whether the gender gap shown in official statistics and reports is factual or a myth.

2.3 THEORETICAL EXPLANATIONS

Much of the convergence debate surrounding the gap between female and male offending has focused solely on the possibility that criminal activity is converging, and if it is, why. Examining female crime from this perspective uses males as the reference category and is focused on seeing if females are "catching up" at committing crimes. This focus results in a misdirection of efforts, of sorts, as there are a few observations that consistently emerge from research. First, females self-report engaging in criminal behavior less often than males do. This is supported through analysis of official arrest, conviction, and sentencing rates. Second, females commit different types of crime than males. They have historically been engaged in less violent crime than males, they are more likely to have a relationship with their victims, and lastly, they have been less likely to be arrested for property offenses than males. Third, these levels of criminal activity are increasing for females. Regardless of whether this trend changes or not, it is important to focus on the matter at hand—that female crime is changing. These differences in criminal typology, rates, and increases in criminal engagement have been explained by both traditional criminological theory and feminist criminology.

2.3.1 Traditional Theory

Traditional theories of crime causation are categorized as rational choice theories, trait theories, social structure theories, social process theories, conflict theories, and life course development theories.

The latter two theories are covered throughout this book, and in particular Chapter 3, so they are not included in this part of the discussion. Rational choice theories are based on Cesare Beccaria's theory of using fair and certain punishment to deter crime. Theorists from this domain believe that individuals weigh the rewards of criminal activity versus the fear of the severity, certainty, and celerity of being caught and punished, and that in order to deter crime, punishment must make that fear outweigh the reward. Rational choice theorists do not focus on race, age, or gender, but instead find crime to be related to the level of intelligence and ability to process that an individual possesses.

Trait theories were founded on the concept of biological positivism, or the thinking that facial features, shapes of the human skull, and stature evidences characteristics of those prone to criminal behavior. Cesare Lombroso (1835–1909), Raffaele Garofalo (1852–1934), Enrico Ferri (1856–1929), and Henry Goddard (1866–1957) stimulated the belief system that advanced the field of biological positivism into the current field of biosocial criminology, which considers a combination of biological determinants and environmental conditions. Theorists who focus on sociobiological components consider biochemical conditions such as smoking and drinking, diet, exposure to chemicals, sugar intake, hormones and hypoglycemia, and neurophysiological conditions such as minimal brain dysfunction, learning disabilities, attention deficit hyperactivity disorder, brain chemicals, and tumors/lesions as the core components of their primary theories: arousal theory and evolutionary theory.

The second core set of theories within the trait school are psychological trait theories, which focus on how personality and imitation, in conjunction with environment, result in pro- or antisocial behavior. Three main psychological trait theories are psychodynamic (development of the unconscious personality explains criminal onset), behavioral (crime is modeled behavior after those such as the media, experienced violence, and child abuse), and cognitive (individual reasoning influences behavior patterns through perception and cognition). Both biosocial and psychological trait theories focus on intellect, mental capacity, age of reasoning, and problem-solving skills irrespective of gender, class, and social standing.

Social structure theories are based on Emile Durkheim's concept that crime is an important, normal, and necessary function in society.

Based on the Chicago school, this theory considers how socioeconomic structures such as the underclass, child poverty, and minority group poverty impact the disorganization, ecology, and strain experienced in society. Additionally, it focuses on culturally relevant variables, such as conduct norms, and focal concerns such as trouble, toughness, smartness, excitement, fate, and autonomy (Miller, 1958). Social structure theories are macro-level theories that do not focus on micro-level variables such as age and gender but focus on race/ethnicity and social class. They include: Shaw and McKay's social disorganization theory; social ecology theories focused on community deterioration, poverty concentration, chronic unemployment, and community fear; Robert Merton's theory of anomie; Messner and Rosenfeld's institutional anomie theory; Robert Agnew's general strain theory; Walter Miller's focal concerns theory; Albert Cohen's theory of delinquent subcultures; and Cloward and Ohlin's theory of differential opportunity.

Lastly, social process theories are based on the process of socialization that individuals follow in order to conform to society. These theories focus on the impact of family relations, parental efficacy, child maltreatment, education, religion, and peers on the internalization of individual human behavior. These theories are widely tested and include: Edwin Sutherland's theory of differential association; Ronald Aker's theory of differential reinforcement; Matza and Syke's theory of neutralization; Walter Reckless's containment theory; Travis Hirschi's social bond theory; symbolic interaction theory; Edwin Lemert's theory of primary and secondary deviance; and social reaction theory. Social process theories focus solely on the process of internalizing society into one's self and do not focus on variables such as age, race/ethnicity, gender, or socioeconomic status.

The goal of criminological theory is to encapsulate the picture of criminal offenders. The theories offer both strengths and weaknesses, and each theoretical component offers different responses to crime and implications for public policy. The main tenets of each theory have converged in some instances to address particular crime trends and patterns. With regards to female criminality, traditional criminological theory has posited three main explanations for why female crime is evolving.

2.3.1.1 Females Are Becoming More Male-Like

The premise of this argument is that males have set the standard for criminal behavior, current research widely provides explanations for crime causation, and because the gender gap appears to show female crime becoming more male-like in nature, the current understanding of research is applicable to female criminality. In other words a general, or gender-neutral model will be able to explain both female and male crime. This viewpoint is based on what is termed masculinity theory. James Messerschmidt (1993) wrote a book titled *Masculinities and Crime* in which he examined the impact of gender on the social context of criminal definitions and measurement. His work presented an argument that traditional criminological theory was created to explain the majority of crime (male crime) and definitions, measurements, and policies emerged from those male-based concepts. This framework is essentially all that criminology knows and the field is operating under the assumption that females are becoming more violent or are engaging in more "male" forms of crime and evidence male-like thinking patterns and characteristics.

Years of research focusing on male delinquency and criminality has resulted in a plethora of literature that widely explains law-violating behavior. Traditional theories have adequately measured involvement in both nonserious property and serious violent crime. In general, the field of criminology has provided validity, reliability, and a deep understanding of the risks for criminal propensity. As females inch closer to the levels of property crime, burglary and larceny, motor vehicle theft, and drug-related crime committed by males, it is argued their behavior mirrors that of males and gender is not an additional risk factor. If current research already explains male behavior, there is no need to create an additional framework or interpret risk factors any differently for females.

2.3.1.2 Emergence of a New Violent Offender

Similar to the movement in juvenile crime that focused on the emergence of the juvenile "super-predator," this explanation argues that women of all ages are becoming more violent. Official crime report statistics show women are being arrested at higher rates for violent crimes such as burglary, larceny, and motor vehicle thefts than they were previously. Both official reports, self-reports and victimization surveys do not confirm this trend with the most violent of crimes—murder and manslaughter; yet, the increasing crime rates in traditional male-like crime typologies have resulted in an outcry by traditional criminologists that there is a rise of new, violent, and dangerous females (Babcock, Miller, & Saird, 2003; Baskin & Sommers, 1998; Bunch, Foley, & Urbina, 1983; Greenfeld & Snell, 1999; Simpson, 1989). This explanation of female criminality also results in the argument that a gender-specific model of criminality is not necessary, as females are simply catching up to the levels of violence demonstrated by male criminals.

2.3.1.3 Women's Liberation

The Women's Liberation Movement began in the 1960s and 1970s as a tenet of Second Wave Feminism. The Movement was a backlash against women's subordinate status within multiple realms in a patriarchal society and focused on social, political, and economic equality for women. This movement was largely led by the National Organization for Women (with Betty Friedan at the helm) and attempted to establish increased education opportunities for women, changes in societal role expectations, equal pay, and equal rights. The movement resulted in more women in the workplace, fewer women at home in the traditional "female" role of raising children, and a stronger focus on the relationship between gender and victimization, sexualization, parenting, and domestic violence.

In 1975, Freda Adler argued that these newfound freedoms came with their own difficulties. She argued that as women were becoming more predominant in the workplace, rising in occupational status, and being freed from traditional reproductive roles, they also began to climb the criminal corporate ladder. In other words, the liberation of women released to engage in both legitimate and illegitimate business opportunities. The Women's Liberation Movement also resulted in new structural opportunities for women in the form of access to funds and power (embezzlement and fraud), the development of "male" characteristics such as assertiveness and aggressiveness as a way of advancing in the workplace, and the reliance on violence to solidify leadership (Adler, 1975, 1977).

The Liberation Hypothesis has been widely cited as the origin of the 1960s and 1970s change in female criminality. Despite its popularity, significant challenges to the theory have arisen, including the timing of the convergence (Steffensmeier, 1978), the validity of the argument for workplace equity (Box, 1983; Maher & Daly, 1996; Steffensmeier, 1978, 1980, 1993; Steffensmeier & Cobb, 1981; Steffensmeier & Striefel, 1992), and the question as to whether or not female criminals identify with, or feel liberated as a result of, the Women's Movement. Additionally, questions have been posited as to the appropriateness of the utilized methodology (Fox & Hartnagel, 1979; O'Brien, 1999).

2.3.1.4 Economic Marginalization

The economic marginalization theory hypothesizes that relative to males, females are under increased economic hardship. Because they are primarily single parents, are part of a patriarchal society, and lack equal access to education, employment, and legitimate opportunities, their crimes of choice (property crimes, prostitution, etc.) are primarily intrinsic in nature. With relation to the gender gap, the economic marginalization theory states that as women have become increasingly marginalized, the crime rate has reflected their attempts to create an income for themselves. This hypothesis argues that the crime rates of those who are disadvantaged relative to another group of individuals (in this case, the economic disadvantage of women in comparison to men) will fluctuate and mirror the economic trends. For example, when women have access to employment, state aid, and support for their children, they will be less likely to engage in criminal acts. In turn, when funding is diminished, employment and educational opportunities are blocked, and legitimate employment is scarce, the gender gap will continue to narrow. Strong support for this trend is provided in James Messerschmidt's 1986 book titled *Capitalism, Patriarchy, and Crime*.

2.3.2 Feminist Criminology

Traditional criminological theory focuses on the abilities of the existing theoretical frameworks and variables that have been consistently related to the criminal activity of males to explain female crime typology and the gender gap over time. Feminist criminologists argue that without placing gender in the forefront of these studies, applying a traditional framework to a change in criminal trends will not result in an appropriate understanding of the gender gap. Feminist theorists provide a few alternative explanations for fluctuations in crime trends.

First, changes in law enforcement professionalism, training and measurement devices, and viewpoints of law enforcement techniques have resulted in a more appropriate measurement of female crime. Essentially, the "dramatic increase" in criminal activity is not an increase at all, but simply a more precise measurement of what has always occurred. This is the fundamental premise of feminist criminology—that the views, measurement devices, and understandings of women in multiple institutions have been fundamentally misunderstood as the result of an inappropriate and male-based framework. Additionally, with the societal and media portrayal of women as more violent, law enforcement mirrors that trend and may be more likely to charge or arrest females as a form of "equal opportunity."

Second, they argue that viewing gender inequality as the sole root of female criminality is not consistent with the traditional criminological arguments that stress multiple variables such as biology, psychological traits, environmental issues, and social learning/processes. They do not diminish the importance of gender inequality, but historically women have always been unequal, so they question how creating equal opportunity for women would result in a new breed of violent women offenders. Important support for this argument comes from intimate partner violence and victimization statistics. Women who are provided equal economic opportunities would appear more capable of removing themselves from violent relationships, thus decreasing the risk factors for victimization, increasing economic and social stability, and allowing for a stronger social network for both the women and their children; yet, violence against women has not decreased. In essence, the multifaceted components of women's lives would be improved through the provision of gender equality and would result in a reduction in criminal activity, not an increase (Chesney-Lind and Shelden, 1992; Miller, 1986; Morash & Chesney-Lind, 1991; Steffensmeier, 1993).

Third, the societal transition of gender roles and expectations may account for numerous aspects of the gender gap. As women inch toward social, economic, and political equality, gender roles have dramatically changed. These changes impact the views that society has on the roles of women (from "sugar and spice" to being equally capable of engaging in criminal behavior), the rise of both responsibility and accountability for women ("juggling it all" has actually increased gender role expectations as females are now primary breadwinners but also work double time at home) and treatment of their behavior (officers, for example, being more cognizant of women's offending capabilities).

Fourth, the War on Drugs and its impact on women capture important components of the changes in female criminality and the gender gap in crime. Since the 1960s, the availability and acceptance of drug use and abuse have changed. Women now have more access to drugs, experiences of victimization often results in self-medication, and more women have become involved in drug use, abuse, and illegal activity such as trafficking. The War on Drugs has directly impacted women by making sentences harsher (mandatory sentencing), creating additional barriers for educational, social, and economic advancement (consequences such as convicted drug offenders not being able to access federal or state aid for educational opportunities), and capturing women in the cycle of criminal justice and victimization at unprecedented levels.

Lastly, feminist criminologists focus on the impact of power-control on female engagement in crime. Despite all the advances for Equal Rights, Equal Pay, and Liberation, feminists argue that the structure of a patriarchal society will always be impacted by the power and control of the ruling or majority class. Power-control theory argues that at home, parents will reproduce the power relations that they experience at work. Therefore, parents' work experience, access to different forms of employment, and resultant social class will impact children's criminal propensity for crime. Explanations and interpretations of this theory have had to account for the change in female activity in the workplace. If either the mother or both parents are not home to traditionally parent a child, this theory states the child's socialization will be impacted. If the mother (who now has more "equal" access to employment) has to become more assertive, aggressive, or dominant in the workplace, that will translate to the home. If women are unable to retain leadership positions in the workplace and work in a male-dominated, oppressive, patriarchal society, family relations will reflect that. Therefore, the impact of power and control will dynamically impact the structure of the family and children's involvement in crime, and in reality, little has changed in the patriarchal structure of the workforce, leaving this variable consistent throughout history.

In totality, feminist criminology questions the use of the traditional criminological framework that has been created to explain male crime. They argue that males and females do share similar characteristics when examining criminal risk factors (socioeconomic status, educational level, etc.), but that the effect and impact of those characteristics must be viewed through a lens of gender. In essence, even the same argument that traditional criminological theorists utilize (that the gender gap is narrowing) evidences the possibility for the lack of understanding of female crime. If official records may not have accurately portrayed women's crime and if it is possible that women's crime is impacted throughout their life course because they experience things differently (emancipation for example), then how is it possible that traditional theory can accurately capture female criminality? In order to answer those questions, it is important to examine the implications of viewing crime from a gendered model in comparison with viewing it from a gender-neutral model.

2.4 IMPLICATIONS

A gendered model of crime and criminality must follow the variables as outlined by Daly and Chesney-Lind in 1998. Those variables are: that gender is a complex product that is not solely created from biology, the ordering of social life and social institutions differ based on one's gender, gender relations and categories are based on a male supremacy, what we know about the world is gendered and reflects the views of those in power (males), and lastly, that women should be at the center of inquiry and not the periphery. In this context, a theory that is used to address female criminality must examine not only biology, but gender, gender roles, gendered organization, gender expectations, and gender identity. It must measure the social lives, contexts, and institutions based upon the feminist model, create a new understanding of gender relations and categories that are not centered on, related to, or categorized as "opposite" of males, and generate and produce new knowledge from a female point of view. The theory, while utilizing measures explained by traditional theory, must be focused solely on females and their unique risk factors, social positioning, and life experiences. If a true feminist model of crime and delinquency were to be created and utilized, it would significantly impact the social understanding of crime and criminological theory, the treatment of female offenders, and the system of criminal justice.

2.4.1 Understanding of Crime and Criminological Theory

Viewing crime from a feminist viewpoint will enrich criminological theory through the discovery of new theoretically relevant variables and the creation of a gender-based model of criminality. Each traditional theory that exists today was created, tested, and analyzed, and as a result, society better understands the risk predictors for criminal activity. The theories have all evolved to their present form after growing pains that have occurred as a result of multiple modes of analysis, improvements in methodology, and inclusion or omission of appropriate variables. Theoretical advancement has a direct impact on understanding and addressing crime and results in distinct and unique public policy implications.

A feminist approach to crime does not negate the strengths of traditional criminological theory but enriches it. Studies have shown that similar offender characteristics exist in both male and female offenders, so it is clear that traditional theory makes important contributions to feminist criminological theory. But similar to the evolution of traditional theories, viewing crime from a different perspective will result in the creation of a new theoretical framework, the addition of important variables, and the unearthing of variables that have not been considered yet. For example, had criminology not advanced from the biological stage of theory, there would be no examination of some of the variables which have been found to be key predictors of criminal propensity (bonding to society, psychological traits, primary and secondary deviance, attachment to delinquent peers, etc.). Not advancing traditional theory by examining crime through a gendered lens is stagnating the field. Continuing to repeatedly test the same models with the same measures interpreted in different manners will result in the same finding—that gender is not important and females are becoming more male-like.

For example, female crime has changed, as have gender roles and gender identities; yet, criminological theory does not measure the changes in roles or an individual's identification with a specific gender role. The measure of sex cannot necessarily capture which gender someone identifies with. If variables are included that allow for a framework that measures how someone identifies with gender-based roles and social categories dependent upon gender stereotypes, we might find that masculinity and femininity are strongly related, or not related at all, to crime typology. How is that factor ruled out if it is not utilized? Similarly, the main premise of the Liberation hypothesis is that the liberation of women has created more criminal opportunities for women. Yet, how can criminological theory measure or analyze the impact of liberation if it does not include a variable asking participants about their perception of liberation? Assumptions are oftentimes erroneous and not enough to base a theoretical conclusion on.

Over the years, criminological theory has attempted to adapt to new forms of crime such as cybercrime and white-collar crime. Yet feminist criminologists argue that theory has not adapted to female criminality, but simply utilized the existing frameworks to suggest that because female crime is increasing, women are becoming more male-like. This is criminological theory's chance to become stronger, more enriched, and a stronger predictor of criminal behavior. Including gender-specific measures such as gender identity, gender roles, and emotional and relational components that we know are impactful in people's lives may lead to the discovery of important risk factors that could advance the entire field of criminology by being applicable to both males and females (male gender identity is equally a factor in an individual's life experiences). If the goal of criminology is to appropriately understand, respond to, and address the crime problem, all relevant variables must be tested, analyzed, and eliminated. This does not mean that criminologists apply only what they already know, but that they introduce new hypotheses, variables, and frameworks. If they do not, the field will remain stagnant. If the discovery of new variables or a new framework for understanding female criminality results, female criminality may decrease, female offenders will be better served by the criminal justice system, and new public policy implications will emerge.

2.4.1.1 Treatment of Female Offenders

Understanding the origin, evolution, and risk predictors of crime allows society to better respond to and treat offenders. Criminology was founded on advancing the societal understanding of criminal behavior as a means of understanding why some individuals engage in criminal behavior and some do not. In turn, this understanding leads to society providing appropriate interventions such as social welfare programming, educational programs or interventions like charter schools, prevention programs for those at risk, and treatment programs for those prone to criminality. If all of these interventions are based on male criminal behavior, society is not appropriately responding to female crime.

Examining crime from a feminist perspective will result in a gender-based model of treatment that will appropriately address the risk factors presented by those that identify with the female gender. It will provide for gender-based psychological treatment, include the internal and emotional components unique to women that have been identified by the fields of psychology and sociology, and address issues specific to the roles of the female gender such as pregnancy, parenting, self-medication, and self-harm. Lastly, if a gender-based treatment model is utilized, both prevention and treatment programs can be appropriately applied throughout the important points of a women's life course trajectory to better aid in crime prevention, correctional programs, and successful re-entry. Gender-based treatment must be applied at the time of arrest, throughout detainment, and post release.

2.4.1.2 System of Criminal Justice

Feminism argues that gender impacts individuals throughout the course of their lifetime in their relationships, their everyday lives, and at specific points in their life course. It determines the ability to procreate and impacts social status, access to education and employment, and emotional, psychological, and social aspects of individuals' lives. In the system of criminal justice, gender is also a highly significant predictor of treatment. Throughout the three core components of the police, courts, and corrections, research shows that women are treated differently (criminal law, policing, sentencing, and incarceration). Research is mixed, meaning that some research states that the police are less likely to arrest women due to gender bias or stereotypes, while other studies indicate that the courts sentence women more harshly than men, and still others suggest that corrections is not equipped to handle men (and research disputes these claims as well); but all of the research in this field is conducted on the basis that the treatment by and within the criminal justice system *differs based upon gender*.

Feminist criminology argues that considering these gender differences within the system of criminal justice does not mean that it needs to treat women differently than men, but it means they must be treated appropriately. To do this, the emotional, physical, and social context of women's lives must be considered throughout the process. One example of this includes officer searches of women. Research shows that a large majority of female offenders have previously been sexually victimized (Bloom, 2003; Bloom and Covington, 1998). The process of searches can trigger posttraumatic stress disorder responses and if officers conducting searches (both non-invasive and cavity searches) do not understand this or are not educated in trauma responses, the women will be re-experiencing trauma but may be deemed as insubordinate and be penalized.

An additional gender-based difference is related to women's loss of access to their children. Research has found that women in the criminal justice system are impacted by the loss of their children in different ways than men (self-harm, suicidal tendencies, self-blame, etc.) and due to the limited availability of female correctional institutions, they are often placed in correctional facilities that are far from home. Not considering these factors throughout the process of criminal justice significantly impacts both mother and child.

Individuals experience the system of criminal justice in different ways. If they all experienced it in the same way, all outcomes would be the same. Each person's experience throughout the system is impacted by variables such as the media portrayal of the offense, the arrest, sentencing and incarceration, the individual's life experiences prior to contact with the system, and all of the statistically-relevant variables predicted by criminological theory such as age, race/ethnicity, social learning, social processes, certain psychological traits, and genetics. Feminist criminology argues that ignoring the impact that gender has, either on the experiences of individuals themselves or through interaction with the aforementioned variables, would result in an incomplete picture of crime.

2.5 THE GENDER GAP AND SOCIAL JUSTICE

The premise of the majority of research on the gender gap is the antithesis of feminist criminology and social justice. Utilization of the male model of criminal offending, criminological theory, and examining trends in female crime in comparison to trends in male crime is an extension of the system of patriarchy and subjugation of women to the second tier. The model of feminist criminology argues that women must be at the center, not the periphery, of analysis. In this instance, this would mean that female crime trends need to stand alone and not be studied in relation to what is occurring throughout the trends of male offending patterns. Crime rates are neither decreased nor impacted by examining them in conjunction with gender, but by creating models that will appropriately explain patterns and trends. This will ultimately result in treatment and programming that will impact those engaged in criminal activity.

Feminists would argue that claiming women are becoming more like men is not a "liberating" hypothesis, it is a constricting one (when male crime rates are decreasing, criminologists do not argue that males are more female-like). Research on the Liberation Hypothesis is based on data that has not once measured female perceptions of liberation. Movement toward social justice would encompass asking women if they feel liberated, if liberation is important, if they want(ed) liberation, and how liberation translates to their lives in order to accurately portray the impact that the Women's Liberation Movement had (or did not have) on crime rates. This is not a deficiency of research that has been conducted, but a limitation of the data sources available to analyze.

The intersection of feminist theory and social justice would also disagree with the core components of the economic marginalization theory. If economic marginalization is determined by examining economic status relative to males, once again, they are examining relative deprivation, not absolute deprivation. Feminist theorists would argue that for women to achieve social justice within the field of crime and criminology, their lives and worlds must be examined as they currently exist, not how they exist relative to males. Theories such as the economic marginalization theory do not include all of the gender-based variables that are relevant, nor do they control for the relevant intersectionality between gender and race.

Feminist criminologists focused on social justice would not argue for a system that caters to women, but one that considers the multifaceted components of their lives. Social justice would not require that the system treat women better or worse in comparison to males; but it would ask that it treat them appropriately according to their needs—not their needs relative to what a male model states their needs are. It does not ask that an entirely new model be created specifically for women, but social justice would require that, throughout all steps in the system of criminal justice, gender be an important component of theory, legislation, prevention, arrest, sentencing, and incarceration.

CHAPTER 3

Life Course Theory: Gender Differences and Theoretical Impact

A woman's life can really be a succession of lives, each revolving around some emotionally compelling situation or challenge, and each marked off by some intense experience.

Wallis Simpson

Life course theory is a cumulative theory that allows for an examination of the relationship between early life experiences and later pro- or antisocial behavior. To some extent, the theory is very adept at measuring the amount of risk factors, when they were experienced, and how and when society may respond to them in order to increase pro-social behavior. Utilizing many components of traditional criminological theory in its framework, life course theory has become widely tested and supported. Proponents of feminist criminology have advocated for its application to women, in particular with regard to the relationship between abuse, trauma, and criminal behavior.

Chapter 2 presented traditional biological, sociological, and psychological theories but omitted life course criminology for two primary reasons. First, it is the most recent development within the field of criminology, and second, its comprehensive nature provides a strong baseline of research that can prove useful when examining female criminality. This chapter will first define and explain life course theory and its components. Next, it will apply the feminist theoretical framework to these components and discuss the importance of considering gender socialization throughout the life course with regard to risk factors for criminal activity. The chapter will conclude with a presentation of established biological, sociological, and psychological differences between females and males and a discussion of the impact of applying components of feminist theory to life course criminology.

3.1 DEFINITION AND EXPLANATION OF LIFE COURSE THEORY

Life course theory is a tenet of developmental theory and it focuses on the onset, duration, and desistance of criminal behavior throughout one's life span. Proponents believe that childhood, adolescence, and adult criminality are interrelated and that continuity or stability in antisocial behavior will extend throughout an individual's life course (Lilly, Cullen, & Ball, 2002). Life course theory is broken down into three main categories:

- Those that argue continuity in offending—there is a latent or personality trait that will persist throughout an individual's life course. An example is Gottfredson and Hirschi's concept of self-control. Their theory argues that by the age of 7 or 8, children will manifest levels of self-control that can determine their propensity for criminal behavior. For example, a child that evidences low self-control at a young age (inability to delay gratification, lack of empathy, impulsive behavior, etc.) will continue these behaviors into adulthood. The continuance of these behaviors will lead to law-violating behavior.

- Those that argue offending can be marked by continuity *or* change—individuals may evidence a propensity for criminal or antisocial behavior but some may desist from that behavior and some may continue on through adulthood. Terrie Moffitt's adolescent-limited or life-course persistent theory is an example of this form of life course theory. Moffitt argues that there are two types of offenders: those that begin engaging in criminal behavior during adolescence (the majority of young offenders) and desist as they age, and those that begin at a very early age and continue on until adulthood (the serious, persistent offenders that show temper tantrums, biting, etc., as a young child). These offenders differ based upon the age of onset, ability to desist, and the seriousness of crime typology.

- Those that argue offending is related to continuity *and* change—an individual may show the propensity for criminal behavior, but occurrences in life may lead them to continue into crime or desist from crime at any point in time, essentially an ebb and flow of criminal behavior. Rob Sampson and John Laub's Age-Graded Theory of Informal Social Control is an example of this category of life course theory. They argue that, while individuals may show characteristics, traits, or risk factors for criminal behavior, interactions with society and other factors at certain points throughout their lives will cause a "turning point," where they turn away from crime. These turning points include positive experiences such as marriage to a prosocial individual, parenthood, or employment. When those experiences become negative, those individuals may turn back to law-violating behavior.

Life course theory is concerned with both macro-level events that may have an effect on individuals (such as war or depression) and micro-level events and influences that impact the behavior or actions of particular individuals (Paternoster & Bachman, 2001). Two central concepts underlie the idea of life course criminality: trajectories and transitions. Trajectories are pathways or lines of development that individuals take or experience during their life span that are long-term patterns. Essentially, trajectories are the paths or courses that an individual is on throughout their lives and these trajectories will be impacted by an individual's personalities, life experiences, and demographics. Transitions are short-term experiences that are part of a life course trajectory, such as beginning a new job or having a child. Transitions that occur in an individual's life course may be positive or negative, and the core of life course theory argues that these experiences may alter the individual's life course in a multitude of ways; in particular, they will affect the onset or desistance of criminal behavior.

The main idea of life course criminology is that transitions lead to turning points that impact and/or change an individual's life trajectory. It is believed that these concepts mediate the developmental course of offending (Le Blanc & Loeber, 1998), do not necessarily occur as a function of age, and occur as a function of the particular individual experiencing them. Each life course theory is a culmination of variables such as societal-level variables (social learning, social control, social structure), individual variables (personality and intelligence), social aggregate variables (income and neighborhood), cognitive variables, socialization variables (marriage, parenting, children, and military service), and situational factors that are strong predictors in both criminal and victimization models like routine activities theory. Life course theory is a true integrative theory; it includes a multitude of important variables that have been consistently supported as strong predictors for criminal behavior.

Life course criminology provides a strong theoretical framework for individual crime fluctuations, different forms of crimes, and criminal careers. The cumulative nature of the theory in addition to its ability to explain onset, continuance, and desistance of criminal activity has resulted in a large body of literature. To measure the full impact and components of life course theory, the theory must be tested on longitudinal data sets such as the National Youth Survey, the Adolescent Health Survey, or the Sheldon and Eleanor Glueck data. Primary foci of life course studies include the stability and change of behavior throughout an individual's life course, behavioral genetics and biology, child development, adolescent development, adulthood, and the impact of a life course viewpoint on public policy.

3.1.1 Stability and Change Throughout the Individual Life Course

Beginning in the 1980s, a body of research emerged in criminology that focused on the concept of the "criminal career." This concept was premised on the idea that individuals could either possess a trait that they carried throughout their life course (latent traits that are either constant or evolving, such as anti-social potential or low self-control), or be on a life trajectory that would head one of two ways: pro-social behavior or delinquency (Blumstein, Cohen, & Farrington, 1988; Laub & Lauritsen, 1993; Moffitt, 1993). Reviews of the literature at that time found that violent criminal behavior often continued throughout the life course (Laub & Lauritsen, 1993) and was best viewed from a developmental perspective (Loeber & Le Blanc, 1990; Loeber & Stouthamer-Loeber, 1996; Petersilia, 1980), that longitudinal research in criminology provided a more comprehensive picture of criminal behavior (Elder & Rockwell, 1979; Farrington, 1979, 1994, 1995; Farrington & West, 1990), and that variables such as the ability to be prosocial, engagement in overt versus covert behavior, and displays of defiance were highly relevant throughout an individual's life (Farrington, 1986; Hay, 1993; Loeber & Hay, 1997).

Life course and developmental theories focus on both the stability and the change of behavior, characteristics, and criminal propensity. Life course research has found that both antisocial and aggressive behavior is often developed at a young age and carries throughout the life span (Caspi, Bem, and Elder, 1989; Caspi & Moffitt, 1993; Huesmann, Eron, Lefkowitz, & Walder, 1984; Loeber, 1982; McCord, 1983; Stattin & Magnusson, 1989), that turning points occur in life that may assuage criminal behavior, such as the birth of a child, marriage, or employment (Laub & Sampson, 1993; Laub, Nagin, & Sampson, 1998; Sampson & Laub, 1995), and that behavior patterns remain stable over a period of time but are subject to change and development (Asendorpf, 1992; Ferguson, Horwood, & Lynskey, 1995; Loeber, 1982; McCord, 1983; Nagin & Farrington, 1992; Olweus, 1979).

3.1.2 Child Development

Traditional theory previously had focused on one stage of life, one variable, or one trait without examining the cumulative interactions of the three. The power of life course criminology is that it views life in its totality, beginning with the first stage of child development and extending until the end of life. Because the early years of an individual's life form the foundation for later development, it is important to consider the impact of parenting styles/relationships, structures such as education and church, and childhood feelings of safety and well-being in conjunction with biology, personality, and emotional components. Issues such as developmental delays and disabilities, child maltreatment, instability in the home, individual factors such as birth complications and hypersensitivity, and family factors such as parental behavior, substance abuse, and harsh, erratic parenting, all frame the future behavior of children and have been found to be related to future delinquency.

The impact of these issues establishes a child's behavior, in particular, temperament and personality, by the age of 5 (Wasserman et al., 2003). Wasserman et al. state that "risk factors for child delinquency operate in several domains: the individual child, the child's family, the child's peer group, the child's school, the child's neighborhood, and the media" (2003, p. 1). They later argue that individual risk factors are a result of both "social and environmental factors" and that antisocial behavior is the best predictor of later delinquency (2003, p. 2). These findings are supported by Dodge (1990); Frick et al. (1991); Gagnon and Charlebois (1989); Gagnon, Craig, Tremblay, Zhou, and Vitaro (1995); and Moffitt, Caspi, Dickson, Silva, and Stanton (1996). Wasserman et al. argue that "the focus on risk factors that appear at a young age is the key to preventing child delinquency and its escalation into chronic criminality" (2003, p. 10). The consideration of childhood development, well-being, family stability, the childhood psyche and temperament, and important social structures provides a strong and comprehensive picture of criminal pathways and trajectories.

3.1.3 Adolescent Development

Childhood development provides the framework for adolescents to navigate the social world. Life course theory argues that in adolescence, individuals can participate in either limited delinquency (meaning they engage in delinquency only in adolescence and oftentimes it is non-violent and non-serious criminality) or they will begin their persistent life course trajectory into a criminal career (Moffitt, 1993). Pathways into this career may include the *authority conflict* pathway, which begins in childhood with evidence of stubborn behavior and translates into adolescence with defiant behavior and authority avoidance, the *covert* pathway, which begins with minor behavior such as lying or shoplifting and extends to escalating criminality such as motor vehicle theft or drug-related crime, or the *overt* pathway, in which the individual begins engaging in serious, violent criminal behavior at the outset (Loeber et al., 1993).

These pathways into crime are important predictors of later criminality. The earlier someone enters into the criminal career, the less likely they are to desist from it. Adolescent development and the trajectory of individual of pathways are impacted by turmoil (Dishion, Patterson, Stoolmiller, & Skinner, 1991; Elmen & Offer 1993; Harris, 1995), substance use by the adolescent and/or their parents (Van Kammen, Loeber, & Stouthamer-Loeber, 1991), attention-deficit disorders and hyperactivity (Clausen, 1991; Moffitt, 1993), parents and peers (Collins, Maccoby, Steinberg, Hetherington, & Bornstein, 2000; Harris, 1995; Parker, Rubin, Price, & DeRosier, 1995; Reiss, 1998; Quinton, Pickles, Maughan, & Rutter 1993; Vandell, 2000), and most importantly, by childhood development, environment, and socialization (view aforementioned citations).

3.1.4 Adulthood

Life course theory is a developmental theory, meaning that no life stage can be understood or viewed in isolation, but they must be viewed as related components that shape an individual's life. Essentially, the person that someone becomes as an adult is a product of their experiences as a child and throughout adolescence. If, for example, an individual evidences behaviors such as refusals to obey requests, temper tantrums, disruptiveness, a hostile attitude, or difficulty with academics throughout childhood and adolescence, life course theory would argue that unless a prosocial institution, individual, or stimulus occurred at some point on that individual's life course trajectory, that individual is more likely to engage in adult criminality, be arrested, and be incarcerated than individuals who did not evidence risk factors in early childhood.

Longitudinal studies conducted with data from the Pittsburgh Youth Study, Denver Youth Study, Rochester Youth Development Study, National Youth Survey, Cambridge Study, Cambridge-Somerville Youth Study, Dunedin Multidisciplinary Health and Development Study, Carolina Longitudinal Study, Columbia County Longitudinal Study, and the Add Health data all provide support for the main components of life course theory. Antisocial behaviors and risk predictors identified by life course theorists have been found to affect employment in adulthood, levels of education attained, propensity to engage in criminal activity, and prosocial behavior of the individuals' spouse (Huesman, Eron, & Dubow, 2002; Juon, Eggleston-Doherty, & Ensminger, 2006; Kokko & Pulkkinen, 2000; Rutter, Quinton, & Hill, 1990; Sampson & Laub 1993). Additionally, adverse or negative experiences in early childhood are likely to result in physical and mental health disorders (Reavis, Looman, Franco, & Rojas, 2013).

3.1.5 Public Policy Implications

The fact that life course criminology articulates the link between childhood experience and adult criminality results in numerous public policy implications. These implications occur from a preventative standpoint in early childhood and from both a preventative and reactive standpoint in adolescence and adulthood. Effective prevention and intervention techniques are expensive, multifaceted, and must address all aspects of physical, mental, and emotional health and social components, in addition to focusing on strengthening the structure of institutions such as family, education, and the economy.

In targeting childhood development opportunities, primary prevention techniques include providing parental education, programming for current or expectant parents that focuses on the nutritional and physical well-being of all family members, drug and substance use educational programs, and domestic violence prevention. Additionally, strengthening the family as a unit is an important component, so programs such as *Marriage Works* are appropriate according to the life course perspective. In adolescence, importance must be placed on school, self-esteem and confidence, higher education, and family stability. Programs that focus on anti-bullying, continuation of prosocial behavior (or development of it if the individual did not form it in childhood), and strengthening fam-ily and social bonds are relevant at this stage.

Life course theory argues that by adulthood, criminal risk propensity is already learned or inherent via biology/sociobiology. Criminal pro-pensity will either be stable and continuous, or possibilities for desis-tance may be inherent by this time in an individual's life. Therefore, prevention programs would not be highly effective, but providing opportunities for pro-social transitions such as marriage, employment, and education would be the most valuable policies to implement. These prosocial transitions may provide the individual support in overcoming the traits that underlie criminal propensity, create such strong bonds and ties to society that it could prevent the individual from offending, form a stable and prosocial atmosphere for the individual, and may provide a turning point within the individual's criminal trajectory.

3.2 GENDER-SPECIFIC LIFE COURSE SOCIALIZATION PROCESS

From birth onwards, women follow a different life trajectory than males. Labeling starts immediately with the provision of a blue or pink blanket in the hospital and gender and role expectations follow. Gender-specific components throughout a women's life course will be defined by the socialization process, social context, system of patriarchy, social and economic positioning, and gender norms and expectations.

Life course theory places a primary emphasis on the socialization process. This process teaches an individual how to act, behave, believe, and think. It offers the individual a value and norm set that will be dependent on who they are, where they live, how much money they have, and who raises them. The socialization process governs matura-tion, attitudes, and expectations, and it is viewed as a continuing pro-cess focused on role acquisition, role transitions, and discontinuity. Elements from George Herbert Mead's theory of the self, Erik Erikson's psychoanalytical stage theory, WI Thomas' theory of indi-vidualization, demoralization, and the unadjusted girl (and Margaret Mead's cultural role theory) are apparent in the life course perspective of socialization—a perspective that places emphasis on expected pro-gression through age-linked roles that are socially defined.

Here it is important to examine the different role, value, and norm sets and life course trajectories that are taught and expected by gender, or what is termed gender socialization. Gender socialization is the process by which an individual is taught expectations, roles, and attitudes based upon their biological sex. UNICEF defines gender role socialization and calls attention to its importance in the following statement:

> It is generally accepted that early gender socialization is one of the most pertinent issues in early childhood, affecting both boys and girls. The foundations for stereotypes in gender roles are laid through early gender socialization. Early gender socialization starts at birth and it is a process of learning cultural roles according to one's sex. Right from the beginning, boys and girls are treated differently by the members of their own environment, and learn the differences between boys and girls, women and men. Parental and societal expectations from boys and girls, their selection of gender-specific toys, and/or giving gender based assignments seem to define a differentiating socialization process that can be termed as "gender socialization". There are numerous examples from varied parts of the world confirming that gender socialization is intertwined with the ethnic, cultural, and religious values of a given society. And gender socialization continues throughout the life cycle.
>
> *UNICEF (2007)*

The process of gender role socialization depends on the social and cultural context in which the socialization process occurs. Young children are socialized by their family, society, educational systems, the media, and peers, and gender roles and expectations will reflect societal change. In the United States, for example, one way to examine the socialization process and the social context of gender socialization is through the infamous Rosie the Riveter symbol. Prior to World War II, gender roles were such that women were expected to stay at home, raise children, not participate in the workforce, and "keep the home fires burning." When World War II emptied out the ranks of the workforce, society changed expectations for the female gender role, and through the presentation of the Rosie the Riveter signs and symbols, women were pulled from the home and told that "they could do it," meaning they could be strong enough to work in the factories, brave enough to go to work every day, and they would still be able to nurture children at night. It suddenly became women's patriotic duty to fill the voids in the American workforce. Without this switch in gender role norms, the United States economy would have not been sustainable during this time of war.

Throughout the history of many nations, gender role expectations and the process of gender socialization reflects the nature and structure of society. Patriarchal nations, for example, will present subordinate expectations of women based on the assumption that they are the weaker sex. Gender role expectations and norms will reflect this. One example is Afghanistan. In Afghanistan, women (and children) are expected to cover their bodies so as not to induce the lust of a male. Women are prosecuted and incarcerated for reporting victimization and rape, as the gender role expectations of a patriarchal society assume that women must protect and save their bodies and virginity for their future husband. Regardless of how that virginity is lost, the social role expectation is that the woman has been defiled. Instead of examining why a male would rape a female or a child, those in power automatically assume that the victim had done something to precipitate the act, and the male is rarely held accountable for their actions.

Gender role socialization and patriarchy intersectionality are reflected in both the gender and the norm expectations for behavior, values, and attitudes. This often results in the social, economic, political, and educational subordination of women. Feminist theory would argue that a theoretical model that does not include structural components related to patriarchy, gender role expectations throughout the life course (both internalized expectations of the individual and societal expectations), and the process of socialization *specific to gender* would be incomplete. If life course theory argues that socialization is an important process from childhood, and research shows that the socialization process differs by gender, by societal structure, and by changing expectations, the life course theory must include appropriate measures of each to accurately identify gender-based risk predictors.

3.3 DIFFERENCES BETWEEN GENDERS THROUGHOUT THE LIFE COURSE

Feminist theory calls attention to the numerous differences in the lives of women. These differences can be biological (based on sex), sociological, and/or psychological. Feminist criminologists argue that it is important to measure for these differences in order to get a full picture of female criminality.

3.3.1 Biological

Research shows that men and women differ biologically in a multitude of ways. One of the most established differences biological between the sexes is the concept of aggression. Studies consistently find that men are more aggressive than women (Blum, 1997; Card, Stucky, Sawalani, & Little, 2008; Hyde, 1984; Moffitt, Caspi, Rutter, & Silva, 2001; Salmivalli & Kaukiainen, 2004; Wright, Tibbetts, & Daigle, 2008), and that the forms of aggression differ by gender, with females evidencing more relational aggression and less overt aggression than males (Crick & Grotpeter, 1995; Lagerspetz, Bjorkqvist, & Peltonen, 2006). This biological difference is one of the components that contributed to the current viewpoint that females are becoming more like males, and that is why female crime is increasing (as discussed in Chapter 2). If female aggression is increasing, crime rates will increase; thus, women are becoming more male-like, according to many in the field of criminology.

Brain structure also differs by gender. Male brains are larger, even when controlling for relative body size. The hippocampus is larger in females, the amygdala larger in males, and males and females evidence different levels of dopamine, serotonergic, and GABA markers (Cosgrove, Mazure, & Staley, 2007). Brain chemistry and functioning has also been speculated to be related to addiction disorders, which is an important predictor according to life course theory (Van Wormer, 2001). Females also evidence more gray matter in their brain and males have more white matter. What are important about these differences are the parts of the body that each difference impacts, such as right/left brain functions, memory and neural functioning, emotional intelligence, and progression of neurological diseases. As the center of physical, emotional, behavioral, and neurological control, gender differences within the human brain provide a glimpse into many aspects of functioning. These include components considered in life course theory such as sociobiological components, latent and psychological traits, and neurophysiological functions and disease.

Lastly, the structure and functions of the human body differ by sex with regards to reproduction and proneness to disease. Females have high levels of estrogen, regular menstrual cycles, the ability to carry a child and are at higher risk of sexually transmitted diseases, both as the carrier and for transmission to children during the birthing process

(Clark, 2006). Women are also prone to breast cancer and heart diseases/attacks at higher rates than males and are at risk for ovarian and uterine cancer (McQueen, 2006). In comparison, males have higher levels of testosterone and are capable of getting testicular and prostate disease/cancer whereas females are not. Additionally, males are at high risk for colorectal and lung cancer. These biological differences have not yet translated into the majority of studies testing the components of life course criminology; yet, they impact the manner in which someone experiences life, cognitive functioning, neurology, and hormone fluctuation—all of which have been suggested to be related to criminal activity.

3.3.2 Sociological

Sociological differences focus primarily on economics and class differences, socialization and labeling, and blocked opportunities. At the core of each concept is the view that women and men experience the social world differently. This is a cumulative result of the socialization process, the structure of society, the social/economic positioning they are in, and to some extent their biological and psychological needs and functions. Gender stereotypes and gendered role expectations result in females holding less powerful positions in corporations, being paid less for the same job (despite multiple attempts at equal rights and equal pay), holding higher degrees than men (yet being a minority portion of those in governmental, political, economic, research, and STEM careers). Despite having strong collaborative leadership skills, communication skills, and abilities for negotiation, women are far less likely to be in a position to utilize those skills.

Females and males also experience different levels of social control by family members, official agencies, and structural institutions. Males are allowed more freedom from a young age than females in the form of curfews, dress code, ability to date, and sexuality. Females are more likely to be socially controlled by their parents, quickly labeled by the educational system, and negatively stereotyped by society despite engaging in the same activities as males (for example, a young male who engages in early sexual behavior is deemed masculine, a young woman deemed "slut" or "whore").

Females' relational experiences also differ from males' social and familial relationships. It has been argued that women are more nurturing, empathetic, and relational than males (Eagly, 1987); yet, they are most likely to be at risk from someone they love and trust than a male. Women are more likely to be victims of sexual molestation or abuse than males (National Intimate Partner and Sexual Violence Survey 2010), domestic violence by their spouses (National Violence against Women Survey as cited in Tjaden and Thoennes (2000)), and killed by the ones they love (Center for Gun Policy and Research Johns Hopkins). In comparison, males are more likely to be abused, injured, or killed by a stranger or an enemy at war. It would be a fair assumption to presume that these relationships are not insulating factors for female criminality; but in fact, they are risk predictors (contrary to the findings for males that social attachment is an insulator variable) and would significantly impact a woman's life course trajectory.

Lastly, one of the most influential sociological components for women is the imitation of power relationships. In a patriarchal society where power structures are set up to benefit males, women that experience this system will mirror or imitate these power structures in future decisions and relationships. This imitation of subordinate status will impact their current and future family life, their choice of careers, and reenactment within the workplace. Importantly, this will impact the individuals' life course trajectories in relation to expectations, limitations, and goal achievement—all key components of criminological theory, in particular, life course criminology.

3.3.3 Psychological
Biological and sociological factors converge to form an individual's personality and psychological traits and capacities. One of the key differences between genders in regards to psychology is the differences in mental health and addictive behaviors. Women that offend are more likely to show much higher levels of depressive disorders, mood disorders such as bipolar disorder, and anxiety and major thought disorders, such as posttraumatic stress disorder, than males (Maass-Robinson & Everett Thompson, 2006; Newkirk, 2006). Women are also more likely to have co-occurring disorders than males, meaning they have more than one mood, thought, or anxiety disorder. This translates into higher risk for suicide, substance use and abuse disorders, sexual risk behavior, and self-harm (Butler & Braithwaite, 2006; Conerly, Robillard, & Braithwaite, 2006).

Additionally, childhood abuse and neglect results in higher rates of psychiatric disorders, such as borderline personality disorder, in females than in males (Bryne & Howells, 2000). These disorders are related to fits of anger, depression, and poor self-esteem (Thomas & Pollard, 2001). They also result in emotion fluctuation, an inability to tolerate anxiety and distress, and volatility. These disorders are accelerated throughout the criminal justice system, as police and corrections officers are often untrained to recognize symptoms or appropriately manage the disorders. In conjunction with women's propensity for internalizing traumatic experiences, social constraints on expressing anger, and high rates of depression, these gender-specific differences prove to be very difficult for all levels of the system to manage (Sorbello, Eccleston, Ward, & Jones, 2002).

3.4 IMPACT OF THE FEMINIST VIEWPOINT ON LIFE COURSE THEORY

Feminist theorists argue for and support the concept of gender differences. However, they do question the conceptual definitions and measurement of the concepts. For example, the biological, sociological, and psychological differences outlined above are based upon the traditional masculine and feminine definitions and points of view. Feminists argue that gender is socially constructed and that the concepts defining male and female characteristics are socially created on a historical and traditional precedent produced throughout the process of socialization in a patriarchal society. Therefore, the definitions, explanations, and measurements reflect a male bias that assigns subordinate or weak characteristics to females and strong, valued characteristics to males. Despite this concern regarding the social construction of gender, viewing an individual's life course and criminal trajectories from the feminist perspective allows for a comprehensive examination of gender stereotypes and their impact on individuals, measurement of gender and gender roles/norms/values, and the impact of gender role identification throughout an individual's life course (Belknap, 2001; Daly, 1994; van Wormer and Bartollas, 2010).

Feminist criminologists call for equality, but not for sameness. In other words, if there are gender differences between men and women, feminists do not call for special treatment or any form of discrimination against men. They simply find it critical for criminology to view criminal activity from a gendered lens so that female behavior is better understood, public policy reflects the specific needs of women, recidivism rates decrease through the proper treatment of female offenders, and gender-specific programming be implemented as a means of recognizing, treating, addressing, and responding to the unique nature of female criminality.

3.4.1 Gender-Specific Models of Life Course Criminology

Chapter 2 discussed the differences between a general model of delinquency and a gender-specific model of delinquency. Currently, the life course model as it exists is a general model that is said to explain criminal risk predictors regardless of gender. A dearth of research does provide support for that view, but the lack of gender-specific variables remains a limitation of the theory.

Unless a gender-specific model of life course criminology has been created that focuses solely on the life course trajectories, patterns of onset, desistance or continuance, and what factors impact life course trajectories *of females*, the strength of the life course model may not yet be recognized. If life course theory is premised on socialization, and socialization differs for females, how are criminologists able to definitively argue that this model has reached its potential for examining female crime? If biological, sociological, and psychological components differ between genders, might there be variables that are not captured in the general life course model that would help the field better explain and predict female criminality?

If, for example, life course theory shows us that having a child decreases criminality, the implicit assumption is that women that do not have a child are at higher risk of becoming criminal. Yet, women all throughout the world are struggling with being able to conceive a child. Therefore, they want a child but may not be capable of it. In culmination with anomie theory or related components, including variables that measure gender identity or gender role attainment could explain why some women steal other women's children or kill pregnant women and remove the child. Correctly identifying and measuring gender-specific variables such as these will result in a strong, reliable, and valid model for female offenders that has not yet been utilized.

Additional variables contributing to life course criminology as viewed from the feminist perspective could be related to the importance of familial and social relationships for women. Research shows that young females are more socially controlled by parents, families, and institutions; yet those individuals are the most likely to victimize them. Inclusion of variables focusing on victimization, domestic violence, and feelings of safety may shed light on the criminal propensity of females. For example, statistics show that young women that run away from home are often running away from abusive situations. Life course criminology would view that as a risk factor for later adult delinquency simply based on the fact that they have a delinquency history. However, without the inclusion of gender-specific variables such as gender role identity or perceptions of safety in the home, we do not know what forms of intervention and prevention may best work, what types of crime they are most likely to be at risk of committing, or the intersection between these variables and the timing of the intervention on a life course trajectory.

Stemming from Kathleen Daly's concept of gendered pathways (1994), and Joanne Belknap's 2001 book entitled *The Invisible Woman: Gender, Crime, and Justice*, feminist criminology has attempted to create a female-specific pathway for offenders. Belknap argued that criminologists view crime from the "whole-life" perspective (p. 468), meaning that they must include all relevant social, psychological, and economic issues that affect women from childbirth on, with particular attention to how these factors impact females in different ways than males. In 2003, James C. Howell focused on the pathway to juvenile delinquency for young females. He argued that these pathways were fraught with child abuse victimization, mental health problems, running away, gang involvement, and juvenile justice involvement. While these risk factors were also significant for males, he argued that the combination of all five of the variables in conjunction with each other impacted young females more than it did young males.

Emily Salisbury and Patricia Van Voorhis (2009) continued this gender-specific pathway by focusing on adult offenders. They found three gendered pathways to adult offenders' incarceration:

1. Childhood victimization that resulted in mental illness and substance abuse,
2. Relational dysfunction "in which women's dysfunctional intimate relationships facilitated adult victimization, reductions in self-efficacy, and current mental illness and substance abuse"
3. The integration of blocked opportunities, self-efficacy, and relationship dysfunction leading to economic difficulty.

Both James Howell (2003) and Salisbury and Van Voorhis (2009) note the importance of examining the cumulative nature throughout the life course of female offenders.

Utilization of life course theory from these types of feminist viewpoints will result in a deeper understanding of female crime and gender-specific policies that directly address female criminal offending patterns. These policies will address the recidivism rates, aid in successful reintegration attempts, and will utilize gender-specific models in the hopes of attaining social justice.

Gender-Specific Programming: Current Status, Feminist Impact, and Available Programs

The significance of feminist movement (when it is not co-opted by opportunistic, reactionary forces) is that it offers a new ideological meeting ground for the sexes, a space for criticism, struggle, and transformation.

Bell Hooks

The components of the criminal justice system are predominantly comprised of males. As a result, public policy and programming opportunities have intrinsically leaned toward a male model of prevention, rehabilitation, and aftercare. The increasing emergence of women offenders within the system has resulted in the transference of male programming to women pre-, during, and post-incarceration. Scholars, researchers, and feminists have begun to focus attention on determining whether or not offering male-based or gender-neutral programming to female offenders will effectively serve at-risk women, or if the omission of important variables leaves the programs inefficient at addressing the gender-specific needs of at-risk women.

The purpose of this chapter is to discuss current programming as based upon the male model of crime, corrections, and criminological theory and present the potential impact of addressing female offenders from the feminist viewpoint with regards to gender-specific programming. First, the chapter will discuss the current status of offender programming. Next, it will present the impact of feminist theory and feminist criminology on programming for women and provide a definition of gender-specific programming. The chapter will then provide examples of available programming based on a gender-specific model of crime and will conclude with a discussion of the relationship between gender-specific programming and social justice.

4.1 CURRENT STATUS OF PROGRAMMING

Current preventative, correctional, and reintegration programming is based primarily upon the male model of offending. These programs address the criminal risk factors that have been consistently predicted by traditional criminological theory—education, employment, socio-economic status, drug use, delinquent peers, and personality components such as anger and aggression. In some circumstances, corrections programming is legally mandated. For example, medical and health care programming must be provided to any ward of the state. This mandate is regulated by the United States Constitution and the United Nations Standard Minimum Rules for the Treatment of Prisoners. In other instances, programmatic offerings reflect the attitudes toward crime and offenders evidenced by correctional administration, society at large, and by the offenders themselves.

Programmatic efforts are impacted by the changing demographics of those engaging in criminal activity. The increase of youth offenders in juvenile facilities, of the mentally ill, of HIV/AIDS and elderly inmates in adult institutions, and of female offenders at all stages in the system of criminal justice has forced revisions in programming from classification to reintegration efforts. This change in demographics has stimulated a flurry of research on the availability, impact, and evaluation of the current models of prevention and correctional programming.

Programming has also been impacted by the skyrocketing costs of the criminal justice system. Juvenile and adult institutions have reduced staff and programs, invested in technological improvements (databases and assessment tools, for example), and are being increasingly held accountable by the organizations that fund their efforts. Additionally, the sheer amount of offenders in over-crowded agencies and institutions has overwhelmed programmatic efforts, impacted outcomes, and decreased the capability for individualized treatment. In spite of these difficulties, programming remains embedded in the core aspects of the criminal justice system from a preventative, educational, and rehabilitative standpoint.

4.2 IMPACT OF FEMINIST THEORY ON PROGRAMMING

Feminist theorists argue that the current programmatic models do not appropriately address the criminal behavior of females. Female offenders evidence distinct risk predictors and the risk predictors they share with males (specifically, substance abuse and low socioeconomic status) impact them differently. If women's pathways to delinquency and incarceration differ from males, then providing male programming or gender-neutral programming (which is essentially a male model of programming that is "tweaked" to include females) will not sufficiently aid women nor will it deter them from engaging in crime. Programming for women must take into context the gendered pathways to crime and include components that address the gendered age of onset (Simpson, Yahner, & Dugan, 2008), victimization such as childhood abuse and molestation, as well as intimate partner violence/domestic violence (Daly, 1992; Reisig, Holtfreter, & Morash, 2006; Richie, 2001; Simpson, Yahner & Dugan, 2008; Sorbello, Eccleston, Ward & Jones, 2002), drug and substance abuse (Daly, 1992, 1994; Urbina, 2008; Owen, 1998), and the intersection between race and gender (Bell, 2009; Covington, 2002). Therefore, feminist theory would argue that gender-specific programming needs to be implemented before, during, and after incarceration and throughout the life course of at-risk women.

4.3 DEFINITION OF GENDER-SPECIFIC PROGRAMMING

Program implementation can be based on a general model (a male model that is extended and utilized for both males and females), a gender-neutral model (a model designed to address and respond to the crime and not the offender), or a gender-specific model (a model that places gender at the forefront of program design, implementation, and assessment). Programs that place gender at the forefront of programmatic design and implementation may also be referred to as gender-responsive or gender-sensitive. Slight distinctions separate each form of gendered programming, but most importantly, each one considers gender at all stages of programming and treatment and can be applicable to both males and females.

In 1998, Barbara Bloom and Stephanie Covington presented a paper entitled "Gender-Specific Programming for Female Offenders: What is it and Why is it Important?" This paper was written prior to the doubling of the female prison population in the early 2000s and appropriately foreshadowed the necessity for a deeper understanding of the women being incarcerated, the programs being offered to them, and the lack of concern and familiarity with female offending patterns. They argued that female offenders differ from male offenders in multiple ways: they are more likely to commit non-violent property offenses, they evidence higher rates of substance abuse problems, psychiatric disorders and physical and sexual abuse, they are disparate and lack employment skills, and they are most likely to be of minority status and a single parent (Bloom & Covington, 1998).

Bloom and Covington converged definitions and explanations from the Office of Juvenile Justice and Delinquency Prevention, the Oregon Intermediate Sanctions for Female Offenders Policy Group, the Valentine Foundation, and multiple publications to provide a set of unified recommendations for programming that is gender-specific— meaning that women and their needs, perspectives, life experiences, development, and potential are at the center and forefront of all programmatic efforts. Those recommendations are as follows:

- Address issues that impact women's and girls' lives, such as development of self and self-esteem, establishment of safe and trusting relationships, pregnancy and parenting skills, decision-making skills, and cultural awareness and sensitivity.
- Do not consider equality to be sameness. Treatment services must differ depending on whom the service is being provided for, include the development of each woman's "self," consider alternatives to incarceration, and build upon women's strengths and competencies as a means of promoting self-reliance.
- When treating women's substance abuse, include theories of addiction, women's development, and a theory of trauma in program development and implementation.
- An effective treatment program for women must include a supportive environment, a safe, trusting atmosphere, and address cognitive, affective, and behavioral components.
- Advance gender-specific program assessment and evaluation with specific instruments and measurements that focus on gender, race, age, gender-specificity, program design and comprehensiveness, and gender-specific outcome measures (Bloom & Covington, 1998).

The premise of their research was later supported by a National Institute of Corrections report prepared by Bloom, Owen, and Covington (2003). This report provided three main contributions to the concept of gender-specific programming. First, Bloom et al. discussed the characteristics of women in the criminal justice system and the way that gender impacts current criminal justice practices. They offered a national demographic profile of the women incarcerated in American prisons. They are disproportionately women of color, in their early to mid-30s, most likely to be convicted of a drug-related offense, from broken families, survivors of physical and sexual abuse as children and adults, have significant substance, physical, and mental abuse problems, be unmarried mothers of minor children, and have no higher than a high school education or GED (2003, p. 8).

Additionally, they provide a well-documented discussion of the relationship between gender and all areas of the criminal justice process. They argue, "If gender played no role in criminal behavior and criminal justice processing, then 51.1 percent of those arrested, convicted, and incarcerated" would be women (2003, p. 13). They identify gender differences in the definitions of crime, the lack of gender-blind data collection, the types of crimes committed and resultant level of harm, official arrest reports, bail, sentencing, community supervision, incarceration, reintegration, staffing and training, and staff sexual conduct. They state "responding to the differences between women and men and their pathways to criminal behavior is consistent with the goals of all correctional agencies. These goals are the same for all offenders, whether they are male or female" (p. 29).

Second, they review existing multidisciplinary research that focused on gender and health, family violence, substance abuse, mental health, and trauma. This synthesis of research is fruitful for the discussion surrounding life course pathways and trajectories. Sociological, psychological, and medical literature consistently shows that there are important gender differences between women and men. In addition to the biological, social, and psychological differences presented in Chapter 3, Bloom et al. focus on the need to study women's unique issues involving medical problems (cardiovascular, cancer, osteoporosis, eating disorders, sexually transmitted diseases), health care access, violence against women and children, substance abuse, mental health and trauma, and socioeconomic status needs (employment and education) independently from the study of men's needs. This supports the feminist viewpoint that studying women *in relation to* men has significantly limited advancements for understanding the complex lives of women. They conclude their review with an argument providing support for the necessity of including theories of trauma, women's development, and addiction theory in criminal justice research, while also suggesting an extension to include relational theory and an examination of the gendered effects of current policies such as the War on Drugs, welfare benefits, drug and substance use treatment, public housing, and family reintegration (Bloom, Owen & Covington, 2003).

Lastly, they provide key findings that must be incorporated in the criminal justice system in order for it to truly reflect gender-responsiveness. They suggest that this revised system must "recognize the behavior and social differences between female and male offenders and the specific implications those differences hold for gender-responsive policy and practice" (2003, p. 75). These key findings are translated into the following guiding principles (verbatim):

- Acknowledge that gender makes a difference—allocate resources to women-centered services, designate a high-level administrative position to oversee these services, and recruit appropriately trained and qualified individuals interested in working with and for women (p. 77).
- Create an environment based on safety, respect and dignity—conduct comprehensive reviews of environments in which women are supervised, develop policy that considers emotional and physical safety, decrease the likelihood of adult re-traumatization by understanding the impact of childhood trauma, establish appropriate protocols and reporting for misconduct, develop valid classification and assessment systems for women (p. 78).
- Develop policies, practices, and programs that are relational and promote healthy connections to children, family, significant others, and the community—develop training for all staff that work with women that focus on healthy relationships, create programming that is focused on the child and connect mothers with their children, promote healthy and supportive relationships among female offenders, and develop community and peer-support networks (p. 80).
- Address substance abuse, trauma, and mental health issues through comprehensive, integrated, and culturally-relevant services and appropriate supervision—cross-train service providers in substance abuse, trauma, and mental health issues, allocate resources to support services and supervision, monitor the environment to ensure emotional and physical safety, mandate training on cultural sensitivity (p. 81).

- Provide women with opportunities to improve their socioeconomic conditions—allocate resources to programs focused on the economic, social, and treatment needs of women, ensure that women leave institutional facilities with provisions for housing, food, transportation, and clothing, provide vocational and educational training alongside skill-enhancing opportunities that will help enable women to become part of the workforce, and provide sober living spaces in the community as well as within institutional facilities (p. 82).
- Establish a system of community supervision and re-entry with comprehensive, collaborative service—create individualized support plans for re-entering women and include resources for women and children, develop a "one-stop shop" approach to community service and use a coordinated case management model (p. 83).

These gender-specific programs must reflect the multifaceted, communicative, trauma-based, and relational nature of women's lives, focus on increasing independence, empowerment, healthy awareness, and provide age-appropriate services to both girls and women (Abrahamson, 2009; Chesney-Lind, Morash & Stevens, 2008; Flowers, 2010; Mahoney & Daniel, 2006; Pollock, 2002; Van Wormer, 2010). They must also include gender-sensitive approaches to physical, mental, and emotional well-being, reproductive issues such as HIV/AIDS and pregnancy, health care assessments and prevention programs for cardiovascular disease, cancers, and sexual victimization and trauma (Bell, Terzian, & Moore, 2012; Bloom, 2003; Covington & Bloom, 2006; Morash, Bynum, & Koons, 1998; Wolf, Silva, Knight, & Javdani, 2007).

These needs must remain at the forefront of the criminal justice and correctional system beginning with the classification process (Andrews & Dowden, 2006; Blanchette & Brown, 2006; Butler & Adams, 1966; Davidson, 2009; Harer & Langan, 2001; Van Voorhis, 2005; Van Voorhis, Salisbury, Wright, & Bauman, 2008; Van Voorhis, Peiler, Presser, Spiropoulis, & Sutherland, 2001) and continuing throughout reintegration with a focus on components of mentoring, increasing social capital, and structured aftercare programs (Berman, 2006; Blanchette & Taylor, 2009; Brown & Ross, 2010; Conly, 1998; Covington, 2001; Czuchry, Sia, & Dansereau, 2006; Heilbrun et al., 2008; Rose, Michalsen, Wiest, & Fabian, 2008; Women's Prison Association, 2008).

4.4 EXAMPLES OF GENDER-SPECIFIC PROGRAMMING BASED ON THE LIFE COURSE APPROACH

Consistent with the life course perspective on crime and criminology, programs must be implemented for women of all ages as a way of preventing and deterring criminal activity. The following section provides brief descriptions of programs that have self-identified as gender-specific and have been developed and implemented based upon the frameworks of feminist theory, life course theory, and gender-specificity.

4.4.1 Childhood and Adolescence

- AMICUS Girls Restorative Justice program: This program is a collaboration between the nonprofit organization AMICUS and the Minnesota Department of Corrections. It serves serious and/or chronic young female offenders. The program utilizes Circles of Support programs based upon Native American restorative justice models and includes family, support networks, and community members in the circles.
- GEMS Colorado: The Girls Empowered to Move Successfully program focuses on four main components: counseling, intervention, mentorship, and enrichment. It is an inner-city based program for youths between 6 and 21 years of age that focuses on education and vocational skill building, leadership training, and self-esteem building. It is the sister program to the Brothers Reaching Our Sons (BROS) program.
- GEMS New York: The New York Girls Educational and Mentoring Services program serves young women that have been victims of commercial sexual exploitation or sexual trafficking and are at risk for developing trauma-based responses. Developed in 1998, the program focuses on empowering women, bringing awareness to trafficking and sexual exploitation, and works with parents, community members, and social service agencies to combat the consequences of victimization. The program offers short-term crisis care, court advocacy, transitional housing, and case management.
- Girls Inc.: This program is a national program that serves over 130,000 young women throughout the United States. The program offers a curriculum that teaches young women how to navigate employment, money, and the economy, build resistance to peer pressure, understand the impact of media images on women and young

girls, develop an interest in STEM educations and careers, prevent pregnancy, defend themselves and maintain safety within relationships, and develop healthy habits and involvement in sports. This program has an official "Girls' Bill of Rights" that denotes the rights that young women must strive to attain.

- HEART: The North Carolina Holistic Enrichment for At-Risk Teens program serves 15- and 16-year-old females by offering mental health, vocational, educational, and spiritual programming. It is offered to girls who need intensive substance abuse treatment, is held during the school day, and is based on a therapeutic community model.

- Moving On: The Moving On program utilizes relational theory, motivational interviewing, and cognitive-behavioral interventions. Female participants are between 12 and 21 years of age, and program curriculum consists of individual and group discussions focused on listening and being heard, building healthy relationships, expressing emotions, making connections, and making healthy choices throughout the life course.

- PACE: The Practical Academic Cultural Education center is a nonresidential program that serves dependent, truant, runaway, or delinquent girls between 12 and 18 years of age. They accept social service and community referrals and offer the Spirited Girls curriculum. This curriculum includes health and wellness topics (healthy eating, pregnancy, sexual health, body image, sexual identity, stress management), interpersonal aspects (components of healthy relationships, the dangers of gossip and bullying, and how to effectively communicate and be heard in a way that is respectful), cultural education and appreciation, balancing a checkbook, and how to create a resume.

- Project Chrysalis: This project was implemented in the public high school system in Oregon. It offers comprehensive services to girls between the ages of 14 and 18 that have a history of abuse and trauma. The students are provided support groups (community and school-based support groups), case management, skill-building workshops, curriculum that focuses on coping skills, cognitive-behavioral components, and information on health and sexuality, healthy relationships, and leadership, and a safe, nurturing environment led by trained individuals.

- RYSE: The Reaffirming Young Sisters Excellence program is a community-based program for adjudicated girls between the ages of

12 and 17 in California. The RYSE program was specifically designed to address the disproportionate amount of young women of color in the juvenile justice system and includes a relational component focused on strengthening the bond between the program participant and her probation officer, intensive supervision and treatment services, such as mandatory life-skills programs and weekly contact with probation officers, and cultural events such as an African-American leadership conference.

- Sisters of NIA: The Sisters of NIA program is a program designed to offer programming to socially and economically disadvantaged 6th–8th grade girls (primarily African-American girls). The program is centered on eight Africentric principles: unity, self-determination, collective work and responsibility, collective economics, purpose, creativity, faith, and respect. Program participants meet weekly for sessions focusing on increasing African-American identity, self-esteem, self-motivation, prosocial peer relationships, sense of social responsibility, and awareness of health issues, leadership development, and entrepreneurship.
- Stepping Up: The Wisconsin-based Southern Oaks Girls School's Stepping Up unit is a residential program that focuses on the mental health needs of young women. The participants focus on increasing independent living skills (employment, housing, and money management), understanding what a healthy and intimate relationship is, and developing educational skills.
- WINGS: The San Diego, California Working to Insure and Nurture Girls' Success program is based on utilization of a home visiting model in conjunction with community-based services. The program provides a girls-only group that emphasizes issues related to self-esteem and cognitive skill building, family group counseling focused on conflict resolution, mother–daughter mediation, and anger management, and healthy lifestyles (nutrition, fitness, sexuality, and education). Additionally, staff working with the girls complete extensive training with leading experts on gender-responsive treatment and attend a 5-day juvenile and adult female offender conference.

4.4.2 Adulthood

- FOCUS Program: The Female Career and Unemployment Service Program is offered to select nonviolent offenders on community supervision. The intensive 4-week program offers all participants individual career guidance from a vocational counselor, needs assessment by a case manager, educational and vocational referrals, classes for job skill development, and aid with job placement (Parker, 2008).

- ISIS Rising: A Prison Doula Project—this project offers client-directed care and education through a multidisciplinary team approach. This team consists of doulas and midwives, mental health practitioners, nutritionists, and parent educators. The prison doula project aims to increase women's capability for successful reintegration with the community and their children. Women that are pregnant, have delivered recently, or have children under the age of 5 have access to a 12-week parenting program and a doula throughout their time of delivery if they are still incarcerated when they deliver their child.
- LIFE Prison Re-entry Program: The Lifelong Information for Entrepreneurs program is offered in two prison facilities in Oregon. The program focuses on building business, entrepreneurship, and prosocial life skills as a means of helping women establish independence, self-sufficiency, and self-confidence. This business program offers curriculum in financial literacy, business plan development, conflict resolution, goal setting, time management, and transitions to re-entry.
- Phoenix Project: This project is a jail diversion program in Wicomico County, Maryland. Women can be referred to this program either as an alternative or as an aftercare program, and services are provided until the woman no longer feels they are necessary. Program components include intensive case management, integrated mental health and substance abuse treatment, parenting classes, childcare, family and partner reunification efforts, mental health treatment for children, educational and vocational training, housing, and trauma support groups and treatment.
- Project PROVE: Michigan's Post Release Opportunities for Vocational Education program offers vocational, education, and employment training. It is a model of reintegration available to women that have been released and are facing economic barriers. The program's goal is to help women stabilize their lives, increase the quality of their lives, and reduce recidivism (Case, Fasenfest, Sarri, & Phillips, 2005).
- Real Women Program: The Real Women Acquisitive Offender Program consists of 31 two-hour sessions divided into three curricular phases. The phases are focused on motivating offenders to think

about the costs and consequences of delinquent behavior, preparing them to change their behavior, and motivating them to maintain these changes and prevent recidivism. Curriculum addresses offenders' relationships, roles, duties, self-esteem, and problem-solving skills (Home Office Development and Practice Report).

- Sisters Inside: Sisters Inside is a comprehensive service available to women incarcerated in Australia's Queensland prisons. The service offers sexual assault counseling, the PEEK early intervention program for mothers, intensive support for women and children (BOWS), a work pathways program, housing services, transition programming, a drug addiction and sexual education program (WILL), and a drug and alcohol prevention program (Crying Walls).
- TAMAR project: The Trauma, Addictions, Mental Health, and Recovery program in Maryland is focused on the impact that trauma has on a woman throughout her life course. The program components are administrated by Master's degree educated mental health clinicians within individual and group settings. The curriculum is provided in a 15-week program, covers 30 trauma-related topics, and incorporates psychodynamic components, art therapy, and psychoeducational techniques. Throughout the 15 weeks, the program focuses on trauma, abuse, addiction, HIV/AIDS education, communication and negotiation, containment, imagery, distress tolerance, boundaries, self-soothing, intimacy, and parenting.
- Women in Recovery: Oklahoma's Women in Recovery project is an intensive outpatient program that is designed to be an alternative to corrections. The program offers aid with counseling, housing, drug addiction, development in emotional, social, and economic tools for success, job searches, education, stress reduction, and medical services. Gender-specific components include support groups for anger management, parenting, domestic violence, HIV/AIDS testing, life skills workshops, and family reunification (National Institute of Corrections).

Two additional forms of programming in female institutions that are based on gender-specific needs include programs that focus on the mother–child relationship and drug dependencies and addictions. Women in the criminal justice system are much more likely to be the sole caregivers for their children, and gender-specific programming has attempted to take that into account. It is important that gender-specific programs for parenting emphasize increasing the legal knowledge of parents (especially with regards to custody rights), increased communication both in and out of prison, and parenting skills such as patience and empathy, and parental warmth (Kennon, Mackintosh, & Myers, 2009; Sharp, 2003). Benefits to these programs include reducing recidivism, improving relational skills and positively impacting life course trajectories for both mother and child, and aiding with mental health disorders and delinquency prevention of both mother and child (Sandifer, 2008).

Programs focused on rebuilding the relationship between mother and child include: the Women's Prison Association's Sarah Powell Huntington House; Colorado's Partners in Parenting (PIP) program; prison nursery programs available in California, Illinois, Indiana, Ohio, Nebraska, New York, South Dakota, Washington, and West Virginia; community-based residential parenting programs in Alabama, California, Connecticut, Illinois, North Carolina, Massachusetts, and Vermont; and residential parenting programs in federal facilities in states such as Connecticut, Florida, Illinois, Texas, and West Virginia (Gonzalez, Romero, & Cerbana, 2007).

Addressing drug use and abuse from a gender-specific perspective has become increasingly important. Both female and male offenders evidence high rates of drug use and abuse, but as discussed previously, the pathways to drug use differ. Therefore, a gender-specific approach would need to consider the impact that self-harm, self-medication, PTSD, psychological disorders, and trauma have on the relationship between gender and alcohol and drug use. Treatment needs include comprehensive, multisystemic treatment models, services such as childcare, transportation, a focus on gender-specific delivery styles (empowerment and skill building for women versus confrontation styles for men), a supportive and possibly all-female setting, and a means of addressing the comprehensive nature of female offending (Mosher & Phillips, 2006; Pelissier & Jones, 2005). Examples of gender-specific drug programs include the: Forever Free Program in California, Choice Program in Arkansas, TC program in Delaware, Recovery in Focus program in Oregon, and the SISTERS and Stepping Out programs in California.

4.5 GENDER-SPECIFIC PROGRAMMING AND SOCIAL JUSTICE

Social justice calls for fairness and equality of treatment regardless of demographics. From the standpoint of human rights, criminal justice programming is offered to protect the rights of all: victims, offenders, and society. The lack of gender-specific programming and the inability of current models to address characteristics that lead to female's criminal risk factors is a violation of equality, human rights, and therefore, of social justice. The social justice models defined in Chapter 1 included explanations of components which may be considered harmful—according to the explanations provided, not offering help to an individual who needs it is characterized as harmful. Therefore any differences that are apparent in crime causation must be addressed, regardless of what those differences are based on.

Attaining social justice at a time when funding is being cut and programs are being eliminated is difficult; yet, ignoring the gender-specific risk factors evidenced throughout a woman's life course appears to be one of the factors related to the increase in female offending and incarceration rates. Placing women in a system that does not consider utilizing gender-specificity in classification and risk assessment, educational and vocational programming, biological, sociological, and psychological differences, trauma informed approaches, or programs focusing on the impact of incarceration on mother and child places women at risk for recidivism, decreases opportunity for successful reintegration, and impacts the offender and the family structure.

Feminist theory argues that the convergence of feminism, crime, and social justice should result in fair and equal allocation of resources for programming. Additionally, this convergence would lay the groundwork for programming models that consider the multifaceted components of women's lives and the culmination of a life course fraught with trauma and abuse at the hands of those in charge of protecting them. An appropriately-designed gender-based model would impact women in the criminal justice system, future victimization rates, the effect of crime on children's life course trajectories, and the increase in female criminality. Allocating resources fairly, implementing gender-specific models, and equipping women to make appropriate decisions throughout important times of transition in their life course will increase the capability of attaining social justice.

CHAPTER 5

Implications and Policy: Integrating Feminist Theory, Crime, and Social Justice

Until the great mass of the people shall be filled with the sense of responsibility for each other's welfare, social justice can never be attained.

Helen Keller

Historically, the lack of female involvement in crime has resulted in women constituting a small segment of overall arrests, convictions, and incarceration rates. Throughout the last few decades, women's crime typology has been changing and official crime statistics show that women are becoming more involved in particular types of criminal activity. Explanations for this change include economic marginalization, women's liberation, the emergence of a new violent offender, and the possibility that females are becoming more "male-like." Feminist theory argues that economic marginalization has not improved enough to denote a change in criminal activity, that women are not fully liberated, that measurement of crime does not appropriately gather the full picture of female criminality, and that viewing female criminals in reference to male criminals is a fundamental and dangerous mistake.

There is no argument that female and male offenders share some of the same characteristics and criminal risk factors. They are both more likely to be from lower socioeconomic backgrounds, racial/ethnic minorities, and have lower educational attainment in comparison to individuals that do not offend. The concern of feminist theorists and criminologists is related to the significant points of divergence. For example, while male and female offenders are often parents, women are more likely to be the sole provider and caregiver, making the consequences for arrest, conviction, and incarceration of greater societal import. Both females and males evidence high levels of substance use and abuse, but the reasons for why they use, abuse, or become addicted are different. Women are less aggressive in general than male offenders and are often caught in a cycle of victimization that begins in childhood. Lastly, the relational, biological, sociological, and psychological points of divergence call to question how it is possible to argue that a general model of crime that does not include components related to gender can accurately capture female criminality or adequately respond with programming, rehabilitation, or treatment for desistance and successful reintegration.

Katherine van Wormer, and Clemens Bartollas debated the generalizability of crime models and presented a thorough discussion of the mixed findings available in the literature (2000). They referred to, described, and extended Kathleen Daly's three earlier suggestions for exploring women's criminality (Daly, 1994). They are as follows:

1. Gendered pathways: Suggests viewing crime from the life course perspective and stresses the consideration of biology, developmental sequences, diversity of women's pathways and victimization, and the culmination of variables on female victimization and crime.
2. Gendered crime: This refers to "situational and organizational aspects of crime that relate to gender" (van Wormer and Bartollas, 2000, p. 55) and must examine how gender shapes opportunity structure and criminal activity.
3. Gendered lives: The concept of gendered lives refers to how women experience daily life differently than men do. Daly's suggestion was to reverse what was the standard of thinking at the time and measure crime as a correlate of gender rather than measuring gender as a correlate of crime (Daly, 1994, p. 99).

These recommendations were made in the 1990s and the early 2000s, and feminist criminology is still struggling to incorporate these viewpoints into analyses of criminal behavior. One of the most significant contributions to the advancement of feminist criminology is Joanne Belknap's concept of the invisible woman (2001, 2007). On page 2 of her book, she eloquently described the denial, misunderstandings, and ignorance of feminist criminology with respect to women and girls as offenders, victims, and professionals in the field. Additionally, she presents the importance of utilizing the feminist method to study crime data. She argues that feminist theory is not relegated to explaining the behavior of women, but that research must be advanced through the creation of gender-sensitive questions and measurement instruments, and that gender-specific research be conducted with the goal of impacting policy and action (Belknap, 2001, pp. 16–18).

The previous chapters have applied the feminist theoretical framework to the concepts of crime and social justice. They have presented research on the gender differences in crime typology, the gender gap in crime, a discussion of life course criminology components that differ by gender, and the impact on programming when it is viewed through the lens of feminist theory. Continuing to ignore gender and its impact and intersection with criminal justice will result in the stagnation of the field of feminist criminology, the perpetuation of a patriarchal system based on the reference category of males, and a deep-seated ignorance of the women navigating a male-based model of criminal justice. Stemming from Daly's (1994), von Wormer and Bartollas's (2000), and Belknap's (2001) calls for a criminal justice system that is viewed through the lens of gender and focused on impacting policy and change; the following considerations are presented with the goal of advancing feminist and criminological theory, crime and the criminal justice system, and social justice for women:

- *Utilize the feminist method to examine female crime*: The feminist method of research is an attempt to overcome the androcentric bias of research and it places consideration on the social context of research. Variables that impact the social context include the gender of the researcher and participant, the relationship between the two, and the understanding that gender is socially constructed. The four aims of feminist research go hand-in-hand with the current state of feminist criminology. The aims are to expose structures and conditions that contribute to female crime, enlighten the community and society to the factors that impact female criminality and propose solutions, empower female offenders and give them a voice to speak about their lives and conditions at all stages of the life course, and ultimately produce social change in the form of gender-based criminological theory, an understanding of females as offenders, victims, and employees, and the proposal and implementation of public policies directed toward women.
- *Utilize all forms of feminist theory*: Feminist theory has a multiplicity of forms and each offers strengths and weaknesses. A feminist theory of offending should examine the individual and interactive effects of class, race, age, social structure, capitalism, and patriarchy. Including all aspects of feminist theory will provide for a strong theoretical model that appropriately reflects the multifaceted complexity of women's lives.

- *View female crime separately from male crime*: Current theory and testing examines female crime relative to male offending. While this has its benefits, it is imperative that feminist theorists view female crime from both perspectives—in relation to male crime and as an issue that stands alone. Theory should be used as a starting point and not always as a reference category. Placing women in a theoretical framework designed to explain male behavior will continue to result in the same findings—that female behavior is becoming more male-like (given the social construction of gender). When crime decreases, criminology does not argue that males are becoming more "woman-like" nor would that be done with racial/ethnic crime convergence trends. The fact that it is done for women reinforces the patriarchal nature of the field of criminology. This can be likened to the field of life course criminology. Before life course criminology, theories focused on one correlate of crime, but after its emergence the criminal justice field is better able to understand the cumulative and integrative effects of life course events. The same could be said for feminist criminology. Prior to the development of a gender-specific model of crime, criminology was able to explain a certain portion of female criminality, and after, a stronger, more accurate, and cumulative understanding of female criminality will emerge.
- *Reassess the premise for the arguments explaining the gender gap convergence*: As part of the recommendation to examine female crime beyond its relation to male crime, the gender gap argument must be revisited. However, it should be examined from a purely feminist perspective. This means that it is not necessary to explain female criminality and convergence trends in relation to the criminal behavior patterns of males. Theorists will advance the understanding of female crime trends by examining the patterns in female criminality in conjunction with related social, economic, psychological, and legislative changes. The argument for convergence has created the platform for arguing that females are becoming more "male-like" and has neglected the impact of legislative changes and the evolution of gender roles and gender identification. Understanding female crime in relation to male crime will not inform the field as much as examining why the patterns are what they are, what the patterns are suggesting, and what they are reflecting about society.
- *Integrate components of social justice into feminist criminological theory development and analysis of female criminality*: John Rawl's

justice as fairness theory offers two primary principles: equality and basic liberties for all, and providing opportunity to the disadvantaged. David Miller's theory of social justice revolves around equality with regards to the distribution of advantage and disadvantage in society. Both theories could contribute to the field of feminist criminology, particularly through the addition of variables measuring components of patriarchy, blocked opportunities, and perceptions of fairness. This could also result in an extension of traditional criminological theories such as anomie and strain theory.

- *Examine female criminality from a life course perspective*: Life course theory has strong components that can provide the premise for understanding multiple types of offenders and why they start, continue, or desist from crime. Feminist criminologists have established a body of literature calling attention to the impact of childhood abuse and trauma, the relational nature of women, and the strength of social bonds and social control for regulation of women's behavior. Feminist theories of crime must account for this in order to extend our understanding of female criminality. An important example of this is the relationship between childhood abuse, status offenses, and adult offending for women.
- *Identify all relevant variables that are significantly related to female crime*: Traditional criminological theory has historically been tested on all male populations or a small minority of females. Over the last decade, this has changed and a dearth of research has been produced examining which variables show differences between female and male offenders. Criminologists would benefit from a synthesis of existing studies and identification of all relevant and statistically significant risk predictors that are specific to females.
- *Consider the cumulative nature of gender-specific variables on life course trajectories*: Research presented in the previous chapters shows that the impact of some variables appears to be the same for females and males. However, when examining the total effect of all of the variables, the cumulative effect significantly impacts women at higher rates. This suggests that for theories to appropriately be testing female offending, scales and indices must be created to examine the convergence of significant variables, throughout what stage of the life course they are most impactful, and how that intersects with the individual's turning points and life trajectories.
- *Conduct focus groups, interviews, and other qualitative methods as an exploratory approach to identify new gender-specific variables*: Qualitative

methods are deemed less reliable than quantitative methods and traditionally, theorists that focus on the scientific method discount qualitative information. However, feminist criminology could greatly benefit
from exploration into the question of what causes female crime.
Traditional theory is limited in its power to explain or account for all
of the multifaceted variables that impact women on a daily basis.
Qualitative investigation that integrates components of biology, sociology, economics, psychology, and women's studies may prove fruitful
at discovering new variables. Focus groups and interviews with
women at all stages throughout their life course could lead to specula-
tion about variables related to onset, continuance, and desistance.
These new variables could either be incorporated into current theoretical models or used to create a new model of female crime.

- *Create a scale or variable that measures gender identification and
  relational variables*: Sociological and psychological literature is full
  of research on gender role identity, gender identification, and the
  importance of relational components to both males and females.
  Criminological theories currently test all models of delinquency on
  the component of biological sex while ignoring gender and its social
  context, perpetuating the myth that feminist theory has attempted
  to expose—that the construct of gender is socially created. Including
  a sliding scale of gender identity, for example, can uncover important variables and processes specific to masculinity and femininity
  that have not previously been considered. This measurement will
  become increasingly important with the blurring of gender lines and
  emergence of transgender issues (particularly within the field of
  corrections).

- *Create a database of gender-specific programming*: Gender-specific
  programming is difficult to analyze, review, and revise. The relative
  novelty of gender-specific approaches to female criminality has
  resulted in a lack of public information on the programs. There is
  currently no centralized database or large body of literature that
  explicitly ties state and federal programmatic efforts to theoretical
  tenets of gender-specificity. This database must do more than simply
  identify the programs and their locations. It must tie the programs
  to theory, discuss how they are gender-specific, provide variables
  and outcome measures, and make programmatic components available for public use. For example, all of the programs listed in
  Chapter 4 self-identified as gender-specific programs; yet only two
  of   them   linked   their   programmatic   components   to   the

recommendations or literature of gender-specific practices. Additionally, information on many programs is unavailable to the public or available only upon request. These restrictions make it difficult to garner support or evidence success when the public, evaluators, and academics are unable to easily access the program's components. Creating a thorough database of gender-specific programs available in jails, prisons, and community-based corrections will lead to a better understanding of program offerings, the ability for evaluation and assessment, and transparency to the general public.

- *Conduct systematic reviews or meta-analyses of gender-specific programming efforts*: Gender-specific programming would benefit from a systematic review or meta-analysis of current programmatic efforts. Conducting a systematic review of all gender-specific programs available in jails, prisons, and community-based alternatives (at the local, state, and federal level) would result in identifying, selecting, and critically examining important components of gender-specific programming (for a systematic review of female juvenile programming, see Zahn, Day, Mihalic, & Tichavsky, 2009 and for female adult programming in federal facilities, see Morash & Bynum, 1995). A meta-analysis can provide generalized results for both male and female offenders, quantify and analyze inconsistent results, and control for individual study bias. Both forms of analyses would advance feminist criminology's understanding of what best works for addressing female criminality.

- *Mandate consistent reporting, evaluation, and assessment of programming*: Few evaluations of gender-specific programming have been conducted and made available to the public. Those that have been conducted utilize different outcome measures, risk factors, and many use weak or inappropriate methodology. Implementation of a mandatory reporting system, a framework for evaluation, and a system for assessment would allow for improvement in current programming, provide a stronger framework for future programming, and would create transparency in gender-specific programming.

In sum, feminist theory has had a significant impact on the field of criminology. The critical feminist perspective has provided an additional lens through which to view female crime, current crime trends, and gender-specific risk factors. Viewing crime from a life course perspective allows for the field of criminology to better predict, intervene, and respond to the pathways of female offenders. Integration of feminist and life course theory provides a distinct viewpoint of women's life course trajectories regarding the onset of criminal behavior, and the continuance or desistance of crime. This viewpoint is translated into a call for gender-specific classification instruments, programming efforts, and revisions to criminological theory. Recommendations for advancing feminist criminological theory, re-examining the definition and social construction of crime, and improving gender-specific programming include utilizing an exploratory, feminist-based approach to studying crime, constructing measurements of gender identity for analyses, and creating a public database of programmatic efforts for use in evaluation and assessment.

BIBLIOGRAPHY

Abrahamson, S. (2009). *Prisons must cease re-traumatizing women: A call for gender-responsive programs that end the cycle of abuse.* Retrieved from <http://scholarship.law.wm.edu/wmjowl/vol14/iss2/6>.

Adler, F. (1975). *Sisters in crime.* New York, NY: McGraw Hill.

Adler, F. (1977). The interaction between women's emancipation and female criminality: A cross-cultural perspective. *International Journal of Criminology and Penology, 5,* 101–112.

Akers, R. L. (2000). *Criminological theories: Introduction, evaluation, and application* (3rd ed.). Los Angeles, CA: Roxbury Publishing Company. p. 310.

Alarid, L. F., Burton, V. S., & Cullen, F. T. (2000). Gender and crime among felony offenders: Assessing the generality of social control and differential association theories. *Journal of Research in Crime and Delinquency, 37*(2), 171–199.

American Psychologist, Vol 55(2), Feb 2000, 218–232.

Andrews, B., Brewin, C., & Rose, S. (2003). Gender, social support and PTSD in victims of violent crime. *Journal of Traumatic Stress, 16*(4), 421–427.

Andrews, D. A., & Dowden, C. (2006). Risk principle of case classification in correctional treatment: A meta-analytic investigation. *International Journal of Offender Therapy and Comparative Criminology, 50*(1), 88–100.

Asendorpf, J. (1992). *Continuity and stability of personality traits and personality patterns* (pp. 116–154). *Stability and change in development: A study of methodological reasoning.* Thousand Oaks, CA/London/New Delhi: Sage Publications.

Austin, R. (1982). Women's liberation and increases in minor, major, and occupational offenses. *Criminology, 20,* 407–430.

Babcock, J., Miller, S., & Saird, C. (2003). Toward a typology of abusive women: Differences between partner only and generally violent women in the use of violence. *Psychology of Women Quarterly, 17,* 153–161.

Baskin, D. R., & Sommers, I. B. (1998). *Casualties of community disorder: Women's careers in violent crime.* Boulder, CO: Westview Press. (p. 192).

Belknap, J. (2001/2007). *The invisible woman: Gender, crime, and justice* (3rd ed.). Belmont, CA: Thomson/Wadsworth. (p. 513.

Bell, A. V. (2009). "It's way out of my league": Low-income women's experiences of medicalized infertility. *Gender and Society, 23*(5), 688–709.

Bell, K., Terzian, M. A., & Moore, K. A. (2012). *What works for female children and adolescents: Lessons from experimental evaluations of programs and interventions.* Washington, DC: Child Trends.

Bennett, S., Farrington, D. P., & Huesmann, L. R. (2005). Explaining gender differences in crime and violence: The importance of social cognitive skills. *Aggression and Violent Behavior, 10*(3), 263–288.

Berman, J. (2006). *Women offender transition and reentry: Gender responsive approaches to transitioning women offenders from prison to the community.* Center for Effective Public Policy: National Institute of Corrections (pp. 1–44).

Bernstein, I. N., Kelly, W. R., & Doyle, P. A. (1977). Societal reaction to deviants: The case of criminal defendants. *American Sociological Review, 42*(5), 743–755.

Blanchette, K., & Brown, S. L. (2006). *The assessment and treatment of women offenders: An integrative perspective.* West Sussex, England: John Wiley & Sons.

Blanchette, K., & Taylor, K. (2009). Reintegration of female offenders: Perspectives on "what works". *Corrections Today, 71*(6), 60–63.

Bloom, B. (2003). *Gendered justice: Addressing female offenders.* Durham, NC: Carolina Academic Press.

Bloom, B., & Covington, S. S. (1998). *Gender-specific programming for female offender: What is it and why is it important? Paper presented at the American Society of criminology conference.* Retrieved from <http://www.stephaniecovington.com/pdfs/13.pdf>.

Bloom, B., Owen, B., & Covington, S. (2003). *Gender-responsive strategies: Research, practice, and guiding principles for women offenders,* Washington, DC: National Institute of Corrections (p. 146).

Blum, D. (1997). Sex on the brain: The biological differences between men and women. New York, NY: Penguin Group.

Blumstein, A., Cohen, J., & Farrington, D. P. (1988). Criminal career research: Its value for criminology. *Criminology, 26*(1), 1–35.

Box, S. (1983). *Power, crime, and mystification.* London: Tavistock.

Braithwaite, R. L., Arriola, K. J., & Newkirk, C. (2006). *Health issues among incarcerated women.* New Brunswick, NJ: Rutgers University Press. (p. 355).

Britton, D. (2011). *The gender of crime.* Rowman and Littlefield Publishers.

Brown, M., & Ross, S. (2010). Mentoring, social capital, and desistance: a study of women released from prison. *Australian and New Zealand Journal of Criminology, 43*(1), 31–50.

Bunch, B. J., Foley, L. A., & Urbina, S. P. (1983). The psychology of violent female offenders: A sex-role perspective. *The Prison Journal, 63*(2), 66–79.

Bunch, C. (1987). *Passionate politics: Feminist theory in action.* New York, NY: St. Martin's Press.

Burgess-Proctor, A. (2006). Intersections of race, class, gender, and crime future directions for feminist criminology. *Feminist Criminology, 1*(1), 27–47.

Burnham, L. (2008). *The absence of a gender justice framework in social justice organizing.* Center for the Education of Women final report. Retrieved from <http://www.cew.umich.edu/sites/default/files/BurnhamFinalProject.pdf>.

Burton, V. S., Cullen, F. T., Evans, T. D., Alarid, L. F., & Dunaway, R. G. (1998). Gender, self-control, and crime. *Journal of Research in Crime and Delinquency, 35*(2), 123–147.

Butler, E. W., & Adams, S. N. (1966). Typologies of delinquent girls: Some alternative approaches. *Social Forces, 44*(3), 401–407.

Butler, J., & Braithwaite, K. (2006). Substance use disorders. In: Braithwaite, R. L., Arriola, K. J., & Newkirk, C. (eds) *Health issues among incarcerated women.* Rutgers University Press, New Brunswick, N.J. London.

Byrne, M., & Howells, K. (2000) Key issues in the provision of correctional services of women. *Women in corrections: Staff and clients conference.*

Cairns, R. B., Leung, M. -C., & Cairns, B. D. (1995). *Social networks over time and space in adolescence* (pp. 35–56). *Pathways through adolescence: Individual development in relation to social contexts.* Mahwah, NJ: Lawrence Erlbaum Associates.

Card, N. A., Stucky, B. D., Sawalani, G. M., & Little, T. D. (2008). Direct and indirect aggression during childhood and adolescence: A meta-analytic review of gender differences, intercorrelations, and relations to maladjustment. *Child development, 79*(5), 1185—1229.

Case, P., Fasenfest, D., Sarri, R., & Phillips, A. (2005). Providing educational support for female ex-inmates: project PROVE as a model for social reintegration. *Journal of Correctional Education,* 146—157.

Caspi, A., Bem, D. J., & Elder, G. H. J. (1989). Continuities and consequences of interactional styles across the life course. *Journal of Personality, 57*(2), 375—406.

Caspi, A., & Herbener, E. S. (1990). Continuity and change: Assortative marriage and the consistency of personality in adulthood. *Journal of Personality and Social Problems, 58,* 2.

Caspi, A., & Moffitt, T. E. (1993). *The continuity of maladaptive behavior: From description to understanding in the study of antisocial behavior* (pp. 472—511). *Developmental psychopathology.* Oxford, England: John Wiley & Sons.

Chen, J., & Giles, D. (2004). Gender convergence in crime: Evidence from Canadian adult offense data. *Journal of Criminal Justice, 32*(6), 593—606.

Chesney-Lind, M. (1973). Judicial enforcement of the female sex role: The family court and the female delinquent. *Issues in Criminology, 8*(2), 51—69.

Chesney-Lind, M. (1988). Doing feminist criminology. *The Criminologist, 13,* 16—17.

Chesney-Lind, M. (1989). Girls' crime and woman's place: Toward a feminist model of female delinquency. *Crime and Delinquency, 35*(1), 5—29. doi:10.1177/0011128789035001002.

Chesney-Lind, M., & Belknap, J. (2002). Trends in delinquent girls aggression and violent behavior: A review of the evidence. In M. Putallaz, & P. Bierman (Eds.), *Aggression, antisocial behavior and violence among girls: A development perspective.* New York, NY: Guilford Press.

Chesney-Lind, M., Morash, M., & Stevens, T. (2008). Girls troubles, girls' delinquency, and gender responsive programming: A review. *Australian and New Zealand Journal of Criminology, 41* (1), 162—189.

Chesney-Lind, M., & Shelden, R. (1992). *Girls, delinquency, and juvenile justice.* Pacific Grove, CA: Brooks/Cole.

Clausen, J. S. (1991). Adolescent competence and the shaping of the life course. *American Journal of Sociology, 96,* 805—842.

Coleman, J. (2009). An introduction to feminisms in a postfeminist age. *Women's Studies Journal, 23*(2), 3—13.

Collica, K. (2002). Levels of knowledge and risk perceptions about HIV/AIDS among female inmates in New York state: Can prison-based HIV programs set the stage for behavior change?. *The Prison Journal, 82*(1), 101—124.

Collins, P. H. (2000). *Black feminist thought: Knowledge, consciousness, and the politics of empowerment.* New York, NY: Routledge. (p. 335).

Collins, W. A., Maccoby, E. E., Steinberg, L., Hetherington, E. M., & Bornstein, M. H. Contemporary research on parenting. The case for nature and nurture.

Conerly, R. C., Robillard, A. G., & Braithwaite, R. L. (2006). Sexual risk behavior and alcohol and other drug use among female adolescent detainees: Implications for intervention. In R. L. Braithwaite, K. J. Arriola, & C. Newkirk (Eds.), *Health issues among incarcerated women.* New Brunswick, NJ: Rutgers University Press.

Conly, C. (1998). *The women's prison association: Supporting women offenders and their families.* Washington DC: U.S. Department of Justice: National Institute of Justice.

Corrado, R. R., Odgers, C., & Cohen, I. M. (2000). The incarceration of female young offenders: Protection for whom? *Canadian Journal of Criminology, 42,* 189.

Cosgrove, K. P., Mazure, C. M., & Staley, J. K. (2007). Evolving knowledge of sex differences in brain structure, function and chemistry. *Biological Psychiatry, 62*, 847–855.

Covington, S. S. (2001). *A womans journey home: Challenges for female offenders and their children*. Washington, DC: Urban Institute.

Covington, S. (2002). In S. L. A. Straussner, & S. Brown (Eds.), *Helping women recover: creating gender-responsive treatment. the handbook of addiction treatment for women: theory and practice*. Jossey Bass Publications.

Covington, S. S., & Bloom, B. E. (2006). Gender responsive treatment and services in correctional settings. *Women and Therapy, 29*(3–4), 9–33.

Craig, S. C. (2009). A historical review of mother and child programs for incarcerated women. *The Prison Journal, 89*(1 Suppl.), 35S–53S.

Crenshaw, K. (1989). Demarginalizing the intersection of race and sex: A black feminist critique of antidiscrimination doctrine, feminist theory and antiracist politics. *University of Chicago Legal Forum, 139*, 57–80.

Crenshaw, K. (1991). Mapping the margins: Intersectionality, identity politics, and violence against women of color. *Stanford Law Review, 43*(6), 1241–1299.

Crick, N. R., & Grotpeter, J. K. (1995). Relational aggression, gender, and social-psychological adjustment. *Child Development, 66*(3), 710–722.

Czuchry, M., Sia, T. L., & Dansereau, D. F. (2006). Improving early engagement and treatment readiness of probationers: Gender differences. *The Prison Journal, 86*(1), 56–74.

Daly, K. (1992). Women's pathways to felony court: Feminist theories of lawbreaking and problems of representation. *Southern California Review of Law and Women's Studies, 2*, 11–52.

Daly, K. (1994). *Gender, crime, and punishment*. New Haven, CT/London: Yale University Press. (p. 337).

Daly, K., & Chesney-Lind, M. (1988). Feminism and criminology. *Justice Quarterly, 5*(4), 497–538.

Daly, K., & Maher, L. (1998). *Criminology at the crossroads: Feminist readings in crime and justice*. New York, NY: Oxford University Press, Incorporated. (p. 290).

Davidson, J. (2009). *Female offenders and risk assessment: hidden in plain sight*. LFB. Scholarly Publishing.

de Beauvoir, S. (1949). *The second sex*. New York, NY: Random House Publishers.

De Li, S., & MacKenzie, D. L. (2003). The gendered effects of adult social bonds on the criminal activities of probationers. *Criminal Justice Review, 28*(2), 278–298.

De Pizan, C. (1405). *The book of the city of ladies 1405*. Athens, GA: University of Georgia Press.

Dishion, T. J., Patterson, G. R., Stoolmiller, M., & Skinner, M. L. (1991). Family, school, and behavioral antecedents to early adolescent involvement with antisocial peers. *Developmental Psychology, 27*(1), 172–180.

Dodge, K. A. (1990). *The structure and function of reactive and proactive aggression* (pp. 201–218). *The development and treatment of childhood aggression*. Hillsdale, NJ: Erlbaum.

Eagly, A. H. (1987). *Sex differences in social behavior: A social-role interpretation*. Hillsdale, NJ: L. Erlbaum Associates. (p. 178).

Elder, G. H., & Rockwell, R. (1979). The life-course and human development: An ecological perspective. *International Journal of Behavioral Development, 2*(1), 1–21.

Elmen, J., & Offer, D. (1993). Normality, turmoil, and adolescence. In P. H. Tolan, & B. J. Cohler (Eds.), *Handbook of clinical research and practice with adolescents* (pp. 5−19). New York, NY: John Wiley & Sons.

Eron, L. D. (1987). The development of aggressive behavior from the perspective of a developing behaviorism. *American Psychologist, 42*(5), 435−442.

Farrington, D. P. (1979). Longitudinal research in crime and delinquency. *Crime nad justice: An Annual Review of Research.* Chicago, IL: University of Chicago Press.

Farrington, D. P. (1986). Age and crime. In M. Tonry (Ed.), *Crime and justice.* Vol. 7 (pp. 189−250).

Farrington, D. P. (1994). *Human development and criminal careers* (pp. 511−584). *The Oxford handbook of criminality.* New York, NY: Oxford University Press.

Farrington, D. P. (1995). The twelfth Jack Tizard memorial lecture. *Journal of Child Psychology and Psychiatry, 36*(6), 929−964.

Farrington, D. P., & West, D. J. (1990). The Cambridge study in delinquent development: A long-term follow-up of 411 London males. In H. J. Kerner, & G. Kaiser (Eds.), *Kriminalitat: Personlichkeit, lebensgeschichte und verhalten* (pp. 115−138). Berlin, Germany: Springer-Verlag.

Farrington, D. P., & West, D. J. (1995). *Current perspectives on aging and the life cycle, Current perspectives on aging and the life cycle* (Vol. 4, pp. 249−281). Greenwich, CT: JAI Press Incorporated.

Ferguson, D. M., Horwood, L. J., & Lynskey, M. T. (1995). The stability of disruptive childhood behaviors. *Journal of Abnormal Child Psychology, 23*(3), 379−396.

Firestone, S. (1970). *The dialectic of sex: The case for feminist revolution.* New York, NY: Farrar, Straus, and Giroux.

Fishbein, D. (2000). Neuropsychological function, drug abuse, and violence: A conceptual framework. *Criminal Justice and Behavior, 27*(2), 139−159.

Flavin, J. (2001). Feminism for the mainstream criminologist. *Journal of Criminal Justice, 29*(4), 271−285.

Flowers, R. B. (2010). *Female crime, criminals, and cellmates: an exploration of female criminality.* North Carolina, N.C: McFarland and Company.

Fox, J., & Hartnagel, T. (1979). Changing social roles and female crime in Canada: A time-series analysis. *Canadian Review of Sociology and Anthropology, 16*, 96−104.

Frick, P. J., Lahey, B. B., Loeber, R., Stouthamer-Loeber, M., Green, S., Hart, E. L., et al. (1991). Oppositional defiant disorder and conduct disorder in boys: Patterns of behavioral covariation. *Journal of Clinical Child Psychology, 20*(2), 202−208.

Frick, P. J., Lahey, B. B., Loeber, R., Tannenbaum, L., Van Horn, Y., Christ, M. A. G., et al. (1993). Oppositional defiant disorder and conduct disorder: A meta-analytic review of factor analyses and cross-validation in a clinic sample. *Clinical Psychology Review, 13*(4), 319−340.

Friedan, B. (1963). *The feminine mystique.* New York, NY: WW Norton and Company.

Gagnon, C., Craig, W. M., Tremblay, R. E., Zhou, R. M., & Vitaro, F. (1995). Kindergarten predictors of boys' stable behavior problems at the end of elementary school. *Journal of Abnormal Child Psychology, 23*(6), 751−766.

Giordano, P., Cernkovich, S., & Rudolph, J. (2002). Gender, crime, and desistance: Toward a theory of cognitive tranformation. *American Journal of Sociology, 107*(4), 990−1064.

Gonzalez, P., Romero, T., & Cerbana, C. B. (2007). Parent education program for incarcerated mothers in Colorado. *Journal of Correctional Education, 58*(4), 357−373.

Greenfeld, L. A., & Snell, T. L. (1999). *Special report: Women offenders.* Washington, DC: Bureau of Justice Statistics (USDOJ report).

Haapasalo, J., & Tremblay, R. E. (1994). Physically aggressive boys from ages 6 to 12: Family background, parenting behavior, and prediction of delinquency. *Journal of Consulting and Clinical Psychology, 62*(5), 1044–1052.

Harer, M. D., & Langan, N. P. (2001). Gender differences in predictors of prison violence: assessing the predictive validity of a risk classification system. *Crime and Delinquency, 47*, 4.

Harris, J. R. (1995). Where is the child's environment? A group socialization theory of development. *Psychological Review, 102*(3), 458–489.

Hay, D. F. (1993). Prosocial development. *Journal of Child Psychology and Psychiatry, 35*(1), 29–71.

Heilbrun, K., DeMatteo, D., Fretz, R., Erickson, J., Gerardi, D., & Halper, C. (2008). Criminal recidivism of female offenders: The importance of structured, community-based aftercare. *Correction Compendium, 33*(2), 1–2.

Heimer, K. (1996). Gender, interaction, and delinquency: Testing a theory of differential social control. *Social Psychology Quarterly, 59*(1), 39–61.

Hirschi, T. (1969). *Causes of delinquency.* Berkeley, CA: University of California Press.

Holsinger, K. (2000). Feminist perspectives on female offending: Examining real girls' lives. *Women and Criminal Justice, 12*(1), 23–51.

Holtfreter, K., & Morash, M. (2003). The needs of women offenders: Implications for correctional programming. *Women and Criminal Justice, 14*(2–3), 137–160.

Hooks, B. (1984). *Feminist theory: From margin to center* (2nd ed.). Brooklyn and Boston: South End Press.

Horney, J., Osgood, D. W., & Marshall, I. H. (1995). Criminal careers in the short-term: Intra-individual variability in crime and its relation to local life circumstances. *American Sociological Review*655–673.

Howell, J. (2003). *Preventing and reducing juvenile delinquency: A comprehensive framework.* Sage Publications.

Huesmann, L. R., Eron, L. D., & Dubow, E. F. (2002). Childhood predictors of adult criminality: Are all risk factors reflected in childhood aggressiveness? *Criminal Behaviour and Mental Health, 12*(3), 185–208.

Huesmann, L. R., Eron, L. D., Lefkowitz, M. M., & Walder, L. O. (1984). The stability of aggression over time and generations. *Developmental Psychology, 20*(6), 1120–1134.

Hyde, J. S. (1984). How large are gender differences in aggression? A developmental meta-analysis. *Developmental Psychology, 20*(4), 722–736.

Juon, H. S., Eggleston-Doherty, E. E., & Ensminger, M. E. (2006). Childhood behavior and adult criminality: Cluster analysis in a prospective study of African-Americans. *Journal of Quantitative Criminology, 22*, 193–214.

Kalsem, K., & Williams, V. L. (2010). Social justice feminism. *UCLA Women's Law Journal*131–193.

Keenan, K., Loeber, R., Zhang, Q., & Stouthamer-Loeber, M. (1995). The influence of deviant peers on the development of boys' disruptive and delinquent behavior: A temporal analysis. *Development and Psychopathology, 7*, 715–726.

Kennon, S. S., Mackintosh, V. H., & Myers, B. J. (2009). Parenting education for incarcerated mothers. *Journal of Correctional Education, 60*(1), 10–30.

Klein, D. (1973). The etiology of female crime: A review of the literature. *Issues in Criminology, 8* (2), 3–30.

Kokko, K., & Pulkkinen, L. (2000). Aggression in childhood and long-term unemployment in adulthood: A cycle of maladaptation and some protective factors. *Developmental Psychology, 36* (4), 463–472.

Kolb, B., & Whishaw, I. Q. (1998). Brain plasticity and behavior. *Annual Review of Psychology*, *49*, 43–64.

Kruttschnitt, C., & Gartner, R. (2003). Women's imprisonment. *Crime and Justice*, *30*, 1–81.

Lagerspetz, K. M., Bjorkqvist, K., & Peltonen, T. (2006). Is indirect aggression typical of females? Gender differences in aggressiveness in 11 to 12 year old children. *Aggressive Behavior*, *14*(6), 403–414.

Laub, J. H., & Lauritsen, J. L. (1993). Violent criminal behavior over the life course: A review of the longitudinal and comparative research. *Violence and Victims*, *8*(3), 235–252.

Laub, J. H., Nagin, D. S., & Sampson, R. J. (1998). Trajectories of change in criminal offending: Good marriages and the desistance process. *American Sociological Review*, *63*(2), 225–238.

Laub, J. H., & Sampson, R. J. (1993). Turning points in the life course: Why change matters to the study of crime. *Criminology*, *31*, 301–325.

Lauritsen, J. L., Heimer, K., & Lynch, J. P. (2009). Trends in the gender gap in violent offending: New evidence from the national crime vicitmization survey. *Criminology*, *47*(2), 361–399.

Lay, K., & Daley, J. G. (2008). A critique of feminist theory. *Advances in Social Work*, *8*(1), 49–61.

LeBlanc, M., & Girard, S. (1997). The generality of deviance: Replication over two decades with a Canadian sample of adjudicated boys. *Canadian Journal of Criminology*, *39*(2), 171.

LeBlanc, M., & Loeber, R. (1998). Development criminology updated. In *Crime and Justice: A review of research*, Vol. 23 (pp. 153–198).

Lengermann, P. M., & Niebrugge-Brantley (2000). *Contemporary feminist theory* (pp. 443–489). *Contemporary Sociological Theory*. New York, NY: McGraw Hill.

Levy, B. S., & Sidel, V. (2005). *Social injustice and public health* (p. 552). Oxford University Press. Retrieved from <http://books.google.com/books?id = peY5Thw1H-IC&pgis = 1>.

Lilly, J. R., Cullen, F. T., & Ball, R. A. (2002). *Criminological theory: Context and consequences* (3rd ed.). Thousand Oaks, CA/London/New Delhi: Sage Publications.

Lo, C., & Zhong, H. (2006). Linking crime rates to relationship factors: The use of gender-specific data. *Journal of Criminal Justice*, *34*(3), 317–329.

Loeber, R. (1982). The stability of antisocial and delinquent child behavior: A review. *Child Development*, *53*(6), 1431–1446.

Loeber, R. (1987). The prevalance, correlates, and continuity of serous conduct problems in elementary school children. *Criminology*, *25*(3), 615–642.

Loeber, R., & Dishion, T. (1983). Early predictors of male delinquency: A review. *Psychological Bulletin*, *94*(1), 68–99.

Loeber, R., & Hay, D. (1997). Key issues in the development of aggression and violence from childhood to early adulthood. *Annual Review of Psychology*, *48*(1), 371–410.

Loeber, R., & Le Blanc, M. (1990). Toward a developmental criminology. In M. Tonry & N. Morris (Eds.), *Crime and justice: A review of research*, Vol. 12 (pp. 375–473).

Loeber, R., & Stouthamer-Loeber, M. (1996). The development of offending. *Criminal Justice and Behavior*, *23*(1), 12–24.

Loeber, R., Tremblay, R. E., Gagnon, C., & Charlebois, P. (1989). Continuity and desistance in disruptive boys' early fighting at school. *Development and Psychopathology*, *1*(01), 39–50.

Loeber, R., Wung, P., Keenan, K., Giroux, B., Stouthamer-Loeber, M., Van Kammen, W. B., et al. (1993). Developmental pathways in disruptive child behavior. *Development and Psychopathology*, *5* (1–2), 103–133.

Logan, A. (2008). *Feminism and criminal justice: A historical perspective*. London: Palgrave Macmillan.

Maher, L., & Daly, K. (1996). Women in the street level drug economy: Continuity or change? *Criminology, 34*(4), 465–492.

Mahoney, A. M., & Daniel, C. A. (2006). Bridging the power gap: Narrative therapy with incarcerated women. *The Prison Journal, 86*(1), 75–88.

Maass-Robinson, S., & Everett-Thompson, P. (2006). Mood disorders in incarcerated women. In R. Braithwaite, K. J. Arriola, & C. Newkirk (Eds.), *Health issues of incarcerated women*. New Brunswick, NJ: Rutgers University Press.

Mazerolle, P. (1998). Gender, general strain, and delinquency: An empirical examination. *Justice Quarterly, 15*(1), 65–91.

Mazerolle, P. (2008). The poverty of a gender neutral criminology: Introduction to the special issue on current approaches to understanding female offending. *Australian and New Zealand Journal of Criminology, 41*(1), 1–8.

McCarthy, B., Felmlee, D., & Hagan, J. (2004). Girl friends are better: Gender, friends, and crime among school and street youth. *Criminology, 42*(4), 805–836.

McCord, J. (1983). A longitudinal study of aggression and antisocial behavior. In K. T. Dusen, & S. A. Mednick (Eds.), *Prospective studies of crime and delinquency* (pp. 269–275). Dordrecht, the Netherlands: Springer.

McQueen, S. (2006). Cardiovascular disease. In R. L. Braithwaite, K. J. Arriola, & C. Newkirk (Eds.), Health issues among incarcerated women. NJ: Rutgers University Press.

Mentoring Women in Reentry: A WPA Practice Brief October 2008. (2008). Retrieved from <http://www.wpaonline.org/pdf/MentoringWomeninReentryWPAPracticeBrief.pdf> and <http://www.wpaonline.org/pdf/Mentoring%20Women%20in%20Reentry%20WPA%20Practice%20Brief.pdf>.

Messerschmidt, J. W. (1993). *Masculinities and crime: Critique and reconceptualization of theory*. Lanham, MD: Rowman & Littlefield Publishers.

Miller, D. (1999). *Principles of social justice*. Cambridge, MA: Harvard University Press.

Miller, E. (1986). *Street women*. Philadelphia, PA: Temple University Press.

Miller, J., & Mullins, C.W. (2006). The status of feminist theories in criminology. In *Taking stock: The status of criminological theory*, Vol. 15 (pp. 217–249).

Miller, W. B. (1958). Lower class culture as a generating milieu of gang delinquency. *Journal of Social Issues, 14*(3), 5–19.

Moffitt, T. E. (1993). Adolescence-limited and life course persistent antisocial behavior: A developmental taxonomy. *Psychological Review, 100*(4), 674–701.

Moffitt, T. E., Caspi, A., Dickson, N., Silva, P., & Stanton, W. (1996). Childhood-onset versus adolescent-onset antisocial conduct problems in males: Natural history from ages 3 to 18 years. *Development and Psychopathology, 8*(02), 399.

Moffitt, T. E., Caspi, A., Rutter, M., & Silva, P. A. (2001). *Sex differences in antisocial behaviour: Conduct disorder, delinquency, and violence in the dunedin longitudinal study*. Cambridge, UK: Cambridge University Press. (p. 278).

Moffitt, T. E., Lynam, D. R., & Silva, P. A. (1994). Neuropsychological tests predicting persistent male delinquency. *Criminology, 32*(2), 277–300.

Morash, M. (2006). *Understanding gender, crime, and justice*. Thousand Oaks, CA/London/New Delhi: Sage Publications.

Morash, M., & Bynum, T. (1995) *National Study of Innovative and Promising Programs for Women 1994–1995. ICPSR version*. East Lansing, MI: Michigan State University [producer].

Ann Arbor, MI: Inter-university Consortium for Political and Social Research [distributor], 2000. doi:10.3886/ICPSR02788.v1.

Morash, M., Bynum, T., & Koons, B. (1998). *Women offenders: Programming needs and promising approaches.* National Institute of Justice Research Brief, U.S. Department of Justice.

Morash, M., & Chesney-Lind, M. (1991). A reformulation and partial test of the power-control theory of deliquency. *Justice Quarterly, 8*(3), 347–377.

Mosher, C., & Phillips, D. (2006). The dynamics of a prison-based therapeutic community for women offenders: Retention, completion, and outcomes. *The Prison Journal, 86*(1), 6–31.

Mothers, infants and imprisonment: A national look at prison nurseries and community-based alternatives. (2009). Retrieved from <http://wpaonline.org/pdf/Mothers%20Infants%20and%20Imprisonment%202009.pdf>.

Nagel, S. S. (1983). Codifying sentencing experience. In J. Doig (Ed.), *Criminal corrections: Ideals and realities* (pp. 195–208). Lexington, MA: Lexington Books.

Nagel, I., & Hagan, J. (1983). Gender and crime: offense patterns and criminal court sanctions. In N. Morris, & M. Tonry (Eds.), *Crime and justice* (Vol. IV, pp. 91–144). Chicago, IL: University of Chicago Press.

Nagel, S. S., & Weitzman, L. J. (1971). Women as litigants. *Hastings Law Journal, 23,* 171.

Nagin, D. S., & Farrington, D. P. (1992). The stability of criminal potential from childhood to adulthood. *Criminology, 30*(2), 235–260.

Newkirk, C. (2006). *Health issues among incarcerated women.* New Brunswick, NJ: Rutgers University Press.

Noblit, G. W., & Burcart, J. M. (1976). Women and crime: 1960–1970. *Social Science Quarterly, 56*(4), 650–657.

O'Brien, R. (1999). Measuring the convergence/divergence of serious crime arrest rates for males and females: 1960–1995. *Journal of Quantitative Criminology, 15,* 97–114.

Olweus, D. (1979). Stability of aggressive reaction patterns in males: A review. *Psychological Bulletin, 86*(4), 852–875.

Owen, B. A. (1998). *"In the Mix": Struggle and survival in a women's prison.* Albany, NY: State University of New York Press. (p. 219).

Parker, A. L. (2008). *The FOCUS program: female offender career and unemployment services.* Proquest Publishing.

Parker, J. G., Rubin, K. H., Price, J. M., & DeRosier, M. E. (1995). Peer relationships, child development, and adjustment: A developmental psychopathology perspective. In D. Cicchetti, & D. Cohen (Eds.), *Developmental psychopathology, Vol. 2: Risk, disorder, and adaptation* (pp. 96–161). Oxford, England: John Wiley & Sons.

Paternoster, R., & Bachman, R. (2001). *Explaining criminals and crime: Essays in contemporary criminological theory.* Oxford University Press.

Pelissier, B., & Jones, N. (2005). A review of gender differences among substance abusers. *Crime and Delinquency, 51*(3), 343–372.

Petersilia, J. (1980). Criminal career research: A review of recent evidence. In M. Tonry & N. Morris (Eds.), *Crime and justice,* Vol. 2 (pp. 321–379).

Piquero, N., Gover, A., MacDonald, J., & Piquero, A. R. (2005). The influence of delinquent peers on deliquency: Does gender matter? *Youth and Society, 36*(3), 251–275.

Poe-Yamagata, E., & Butts, J. A. (1996). *Female offenders in the juvenile justice system: Statistics summary.* Diane Publishing Company. (p. 25).

Pollock, J. M. (2002). *Women, prison and crime.* Belmont, CA: Wadsworth Thomson Learning.

Quinton, D., Pickles, A., Maughan, B., & Rutter, M. (1993). Partners, peers, and pathways: Assortative pairing and continuities in conduct disorder. *Development and Psychopathology, 5,* 763–783.

Rafter, N. H. (1985). *Partial justice: Women in state Prisons, 1800–1935.* Boston, MA: Northeastern University Press.

Rasche, C. E. (1974). The female offender as an object of criminological research. *Criminal Justice and Behavior, 1*(4), 301–320.

Rawls, J. (1971). *A theory of justice.* New York, NY: Oxford University Press.

Reavis, J. A., Looman, J., Franco, K. A., & Rojas, B. (2013). Adverse childhood experiences and adult criminality: How long must we live before we possess our own lives? *The Permanente Journal, 17*(2), 44–48.

Reckdenwald, A., & Parker, K. F. (2008). The influence of gender inequality and marginalization on types of female offending. *Homicide Studies, 12,* 208–226.

Reisig, M. D., Holtfreter, K., & Morash, M. (2006). Assessing recidivism risk across female pathways to crime. *Justice Quarterly, 23*(3), 384–405.

Reiss, A. J., Jr (1988). Co-offending and criminal careers. In M. Tonry, & N. Morris (Eds.), *Crime and justice: A review of research (Vol. 10,* pp. 117–170). Chicago, IL: University of Chicago Press.

Richie, B. E. (2001). Challenges incarcerated women face as they return to their communities: Findings from life history interviews. *Crime and Delinquency, 47*(3), 368–389.

Rose, D. R., Michalsen, V., Wiest, D. R., & Fabian, A. (2008). *Women, re-entry and everyday life: Time to work?* (pp. 1–190). Retrieved from <http://www.wpaonline.org/pdf/Women%20Reentry%20and%20Everyday%20Life%20-%20Final%20Report.pdf>.

Rutter, M., Quinton, D., & Hill, J. (1990). Adult outcome of institution-reared children: Males and females compared. In L. N. Robins, & M. Rutter (Eds.), *Straight and devious pathways from childhood to adulthood* (pp. 135–157). New York, NY: Cambridge University Press.

Salisbury, E. J., & Van Voorhis, P. (2009). Gendered pathways: A quantitative investigation of women probationers' paths to incarceration. *Criminal Justice and Behavior, 36*(6), 541–566.

Salmivalli, C., & Kaukiainen, A. (2004). "Female aggression" revisited: Variable-and person-centered approaches to studying gender differences in different types of aggression. *Aggressive Behavior, 30*(2), 158–163.

Sampson, R. J., & Laub, J. H. (1990). Crime and deviance over the life course: The salience of adult social binds. *American Sociological Review, 55,* 609–627.

Sampson, R. J., & Laub, J. H. (1992). Crime and deviance in the life course. *Annual Review of Sociology, 18,* 63–84.

Sampson, R. J., & Laub, J. H. (1993). Structural variations in juvenile court processing: Inequality, the underclass, and social control. *Law and Society Review, 27*(2), 285–311.

Sampson, R. J., & Laub, J. H. (1995). Understanding variability in lives through time: Contributions of life-course criminology. *Studies on Crime and Crime Prevention, 4,* 143–158.

Sandifer, J. L. (2008). Evaluating the efficacy of a parenting program for incarcerated mothers. *The Prison Journal, 88*(3), 423–445.

Schlossman, S., & Wallach, S. (1978). The crime of precocious sexuality: Female juvenile delinquency in the progressive era. *Harvard Educational Review, 48*(1), 65–94.

Schwartz, J. (1996). Gender differences in drunk driving prevalence rates and trends: A 20 year assessment using multiple sources of evidence. *Addictive Behaviors, 9,* 1217–1222.

Schwartz, J. (2008). Gender differences in homicide offending. In M. DeLisi, & P. Conis (Eds.), *Violent offenders: theory, research, public policy, and practice.* Boston: Jones &Bartlett.

Schwartz, J., & Rookey, B. D. (2008). The narrowing gender gap in arrests: Assessing competing explanations using self-report, traffic fatality, and official data on drunk driving, 1980–2004. *Criminology, 46*(3), 637–671.

Schwartz, J., Steffensmeier, D., Zhong, H., & Ackerman, J. (2009). Trends in the gender gap in violence: Reevaluating NCVS and other evidence. *Criminology, 47*(2), 701–724.

Schwartz, M. D., & Milovanovic, D. (1999). In M. D. Schwartz, & D. Milovanovic (Eds.), *Race, gender, and class in criminology: The intersections*. New York, NY: Garland Publishing.

Sharp, S. F. (2003). *Mothers in prison: Issues in parent-child contact* (pp. 151–166). *The incarcerated woman: Rehabilitative programming in women's prisons*. Upper Saddle River, NJ: Prentice Hall.

Sharp, S. F., & Muraskin, R. (2003). *The incarcerated woman: Rehabilitative programming in women's prisons*. Upper Saddle River, NJ: Prentice Hall.

Simon, R. J. (1975). *Women and crime*. New York, NY: Lexington Books. (p. 142).

Simons, R. L., Johnson, C., Conger, R. D., & Elder, G. (1998). A test of latent trait versus life course perspectives on the stability of adolescent antisocial behavior. *Criminology, 36*(2), 217–244.

Simpson, S. S. (1989). Feminist theory, crime and justice. *Criminology, 27*(4), 605–632.

Simpson, S. S., Yahner, J. L., & Dugan, L. (2008). Understanding women's pathways to jail: Analysing the lives of incarcerated women. *Australian and New Zealand Journal of Criminology, 41*(1), 84–108.

Smart, C. (1976). *Women, crime and criminology: A feminist critique*. London: Routledge and Kegan Paul.

Sokoloff, N. J., & Dupont, I. (2005). Domestic violence at the intersections of race, class, and gender challenges and contributions to understanding violence against marginalized women in diverse. *Violence Against Women, 11*(1), 38–64.

Sorbello, L., Eccleston, L., Ward, T., & Jones, R. (2002). Treatment needs of female offenders: A review. *Australian Psychologist, 37*(3), 198–205.

Stattin, H., & Magnusson, D. (1989). The role of early aggressive behavior in the frequency, seriousness, and types of later crimes. *Journal of Consulting and Clinical Psychology, 57*(6), 710–718.

Stattin, H., & Magnusson, D. (1991). Stability and change in criminal behavior up to age 30. *British Journal of Criminology, 31*, 327–346.

Steffensmeier, D., & Allan, E. (1996). Gender and crime: Toward a gendered theory of female offending. *Annual Review of Sociology, 22*(1), 459–487.

Steffensmeier, D., Schwartz, J., Zhong, H., & Ackerman, J. (2005). An assessment of recent trends in girls' violence using diverse longitudinal sources: Is the gender gap closing? *Criminology, 43*(2), 355–406.

Steffensmeier, D., & Streifel, C. (1992). Time-series analysis of the female percentage of arrests for property crimes, 1960–1985: A test of alternative explanations. *Justice Quarterly, 9*(1), 77–103.

Steffensmeier, D. J. (1978). Crime and the contemporary woman: An analysis of changing levels of property crime, 1960–75. *Social Forces, 57*, 566–584.

Steffensmeier, D. J. (1980). A review and assessment of sex differences in adult crime, 1965–77. *Social Forces, 58*, 1080–1108.

Steffensmeier, D. J. (1993). National trends in female arrests, 1960–1990: Assessment and recommendations for research. *Journal of Quantitative Criminology, 9*, 413–441.

Steffensmeier, D. J., & Cobb, M. J. (1981). Sex differences in urban arrest patterns, 1934–79. *Social Problems, 29*(1), 37–50.

Stopes, M. C. (1918). *Married love: Or love in marriage*. New York, NY: The Critic and Guide Company.

Thomas, A., & Pollard, J. (2001). *Substance abuse, trauma, and coping: A report on women prisoners at the Dame Phyllis Frost Centre for women*. Cariniche Pvt. Limited.

Tibbetts, S. G., & Piquero, A. R. (1999). The influence of gender, low birthweight, and disadvantaged environment in predicting early onset of offending: A test of Moffitt's interactional hypothesis. *Criminology, 37*(4), 843–878.

Tjaden, P., & Thoennes, N. (2000). *Full report of the prevalence, incidence, and consequencesof violence against women: Findings from the national violence against women survey*. Washington, DC: National Institute of Justice. Retrieved from <https://www.ncjrs.gov/pdffiles1/nij/183781.pdf>.

Urbina, M. G. (2008). *A comprehensive study of female offenders: Life before, during and after incarceration*. Springfield, IL: Charles C. Thomas Publisher, Ltd..

Van Kammen, W. B. (1991). Substance use and its relationship to conduct problems and delinquency in young boys. *Journal of Youth and Adolescence, 20*(4), 399–413.

Van Kammen, W. B., Loeber, R., & Stouthamer-Loeber, M. (1991). Substance use and its relationship to antisocial and delinquent behavior in young boys. *Journal of Youth and Adolescence, 20*, 399–414.

Van Voorhis, P. (2005). Classification of women offenders: Gender-responsive approaches to risk/needs assessment. *Community Corrections Report, 12*(2), 19–20.

Van Voorhis, P., Peiler, J., Presser, L., Spiropoulis, G., & Sutherland, J. (2001). *Classification of women offenders: A national assessment of current practices and the experiences of three states*. Washington, DC: National Institute of Corrections.

Van Voorhis, P., Salisbury, E., Wright, E., & Bauman, A. (2007). Research note: A new classification instrument for female offenders. *Corrections Today, 96–97*.

Van Voorhis, P., Salisbury, E. J., Wright, E. M., & Bauman, A. (2008). *Achieving accurate pictures of risk and identifying gender-responsive needs: two new assessments for women offenders*. Washington, DC: National Institute of Corrections, United States, Department of Justice.

Van Wormer, K. (2010). *Working with female offenders: A gender sensitive approach*. Hoboken, NJ: John Wiley & Sons.

Van Wormer, K. S. (2001). *Counseling female offenders and victims: A strengths-restorative approach*. New York, NY: Springer Publishing Co. (p. 377).

Van Wormer, K. S., & Bartollas, C. (2010). *Women and the criminal justice system* (3rd ed.) Upper Saddle River, NJ: Prentice Hall PTR. (p. 409).

Vandell, D. L. (2000). Parents, peer groups, and other socializing influences. *Developmental Psychology, 36*(6), 699–710.

Visher, C. A. (1983). Gender, police arrest decisions, and notions of chivalry. *Criminology, 21*(1), 5–28.

Voices from the field: Findings from the NGI listening sessions. (2012). (pp. 1–32). National Girls Institute. Retrieved from: <http://www.nationalgirlsinstitute.org/wp-content/uploads/2012/09/NGI-Listening-Sessions-report.pdf>.

Warr, M. (1998). Life-course transitions and desistance from crime. *Criminology, 36*(2), 183–216.

Wasserman, G. A., Keenan, K., Tremblay, R. E., Coie, J. D., Herrenkohl, T. I., Loeber, R., & et al. (2003). *Risk and protectivefactors of child delinquency* (pp. 1–15). US Department of Justice. Available at: <https://www.ncjrs.gov/pdffiles1/ojjdp/193409.pdf>.

White, K. (2008). Women in federal prison: Pathways in, programs out. *William & Mary Journal of Women and the Law, 14*(2), 305–318.

Williams, J. E., & Best, D. L. (1990). *Sex and psyche: gender and self viewed cross-culturally*. Newbury Park, CA: Sage.

Wittig, M. (1992). *The straight mind: And other essays*. Boston, MA: Beacon Press.

Wolf, A. M., Silva, F., Knight, K. E., & Javdani, S. (2007). Responding to the health needs of female offenders. In R. Sheehan, G. McIvor, & C. Trotter (Eds.), *What works with women offenders* (pp. 182–213). Devon, UK: Willan Publishing.

Wolstonecraft, M. (1792). *A vindication of the rights of woman: With strictures on moral and political subjects*. Boston, MA: Thomas and Andrews.

Women's Prison association: A report on the first ten years of the Sarah Powell Huntington house. (n.d.). (pp. 1–16). Women's Prison Association. Available at: <http://www.wpaonline.org/pdf/SPHH_Report.pdf>.

Women's Prison Association. (2008). Addressing women's incarceration: a national survey of state commissions and task forces on women in the criminal justice system. Institution on Women and Criminal Justice Report.

Wright, J. P., Tibbetts, S. G., & Daigle, L. E. (2008). *Criminals in the making: Criminality across the life course*. Los Angeles, CA: Sage Publications.

Zahn, M. A., Day, J. C., Mihalic, S. F., & Tichavsky, L. (2009). Determining what works for girls in the juvenile justice system: A summary of evaluation evidence. *Crime and Delinquency, 55* (2), 266–293.

Zaplin, R. (2008). *Female offenders: Critical perspectives and effective interventions* (2nd ed.). Sudbury, MA: Jones & Bartlett Learning. p. 622.

Zimmerman, G. M., & Messner, S. S. (2010). Neighborhood context and the gender gap in adolescent violent crime. *American Sociological Review, 75*(6), 958–980.